Dealing with A Narcissistic Personality

A Guide to Surviving A Narcissistic Relationship

BY

Stephen Nico Williams

Dedicated To All Victims of Narcissistic Abuse

Table of Contents

Introduction

Congratulations, and thank you for reading this book on, '**Dealing with a Narcissistic Personality Disorder.**'

If you are considering entering into a relationship with someone who has narcissistic tendencies, you must understand what you are getting yourself into. That's because the biggest problem with dealing with a narcissistic personality is that the disorder is often difficult to diagnose. Many people who have a narcissistic personality disorder are able to charm and manipulate those around them into believing that they are actually very kind, caring, and sensitive people. This can make it difficult for friends, family members, and coworkers to understand that there is actually a problem.

This book will therefore help you to identify if your relationship is toxic and, if it is, provides practical coping strategies for living with a narcissist. If you decide to walk away and leave the relationship, the book also describes how to survive and thrive after the breakup. With real-life examples of narcissistic situations, this book provides essential information for anyone who wants to protect themselves from being sucked in by a narcissist.

Why Read this Book?

This book can help someone in a relationship with a narcissist identify if their relationship is toxic. In it, the author explains, in great detail, the narcissistic personality disorder and how to identify it in different settings. The numerous real-life stories will assist you in identifying character traits in a romantic partner, a spouse, a child, a boss, a coworker or a friend that has these tendencies.

If someone is in a relationship with a narcissist, the book also provides practical coping strategies for living with them. If they choose to leave the relationship, the book offers guidance on how to rebuild their life. You will also get support resources and advise on how to help a friend in a toxic relationship.

This Book Is Best for Those Who Want To:

1). Better understand narcissistic personality disorder.

2). Know how to cope and leave a toxic relationship with a Narcissist.

3). Know how to regain back their life after a toxic relationship with a Narcissist.

4). Be able to enjoy my life without having to worry about a narcissistic personality relationship.

5). Are ready to get rid of the narcissistic relationship in their lives and are looking for supportive groups and coaches for help.

6). Help a close friend with getting out of a toxic relationship.

What You Will Find in The Book:

1. The book explains in-depth what a narcissistic personality disorder is and how to identify one.

2. The book offers practical coping strategies for living with a narcissist, whether you decide to stay or walk away from the relationship.

3. The book features real-life examples of narcissistic situations of toxic relationships and stories of those who have survived them.

4. The book gives advice on how to survive and thrive after the relationship, should you decide to leave it.

5. The book explains how to support a friend who may be in a toxic relationship.

6. The book provides resources of where to find help and support after being a narcissistic relationship.

So, if you are struggling with a narcissistic personality disorder relationship, read this life changing book today!

Chapter 1: What is A Narcissistic Personality Disorder (NPD)?

The word "narcissism" originated from a Greek tale of a handsome young man called Narcissus, a dashing sixteen-year-old lad who fell in love with his own reflection in a pool. According to the Greek Mythology, this is how the tale goes;

> *"Narcissus had never loved anyone as much as he loved his reflection upon seeing his face staring back at him in a pond. Meanwhile, Echo, a young mountain girl, had been cursed by the Goddess Hera and could only speak the words that she had last heard. Echo saw Narcissus and was captivated by his beauty, but she could not express her feelings for him because she could not speak. She followed him until he noticed his reflection in the water, and then she heard him speak. Infatuated with his reflection, Narcissus said, "You are the picture of perfection." Hearing his words, Echo repeated, "You are the picture of perfection." Narcissus, thrilled by the reassurance he received from what he assumed was his reflection speaking back to him, continued, "I've never said this to anyone, but I believe I love you." Echo repeated his words once more, "I love you." Narcissus' love for himself became stronger due to the reciprocated appreciation. As he continued to praise his reflection, and "his reflection" (Echo) continued to reciprocate the praise, Narcissus was utterly overcome by the addictive feeling this pseudo-love provided. In the end, Narcissus became so obsessed with himself that he perished in the pond while attempting to kiss his image, and Echo was left, heartbroken and alone, to wander the hills and caves of the valley, never to love again.*

> *Story adapted from Atsma*

The Narcissistic personality disorder (NPD) is therefore a pervasive pattern of grandiosity (in behavior or pattern), a strong need to be admired by others, and an unapologetic lack of empathy for others. NPD manifests itself in early adulthood, but children can also display it.

Someone with a narcissistic personality disorder has an overinflated ego, tends to place their needs before others, and often manipulates people or situations to ensure they receive what they want. Narcissists value admiration and validation- these are crucial parts of their identity, and they can collapse or become depressed when these needs are unmet. As a result, they typically experience difficulties in their interpersonal relationships.

How To Spot Someone With NPD?

NPD is also referred to as a personality disorder with a consistent pattern of behavior, and inner experience is pervasive and inflexible. Those with a narcissistic personality disorder have a condescending aura, a superiority complex, a lack of empathy, and strong self-admiration. These individuals also value physical pleasure more than emotional intimacy in their sexual relations. Narcissistic individuals have a general false concept of self, and their narcissistic character is a shield that masks their underlying vulnerabilities.

Here are some characteristics of a typical Narcissist;

1. Their online presence is flawless.

Narcissists capitalize on social media to sell their image and self-perceived likable qualities to others. They get more satisfaction with every "like" they get. They never put-up bad pictures and always look polished. All their days always seem perfect. From dinner with the family to lunch with their partners or spouses, everything always appears rosy.

2. They are pay no attention to others, and prefer to be heard.

With a narcissist, there is no such thing as a balanced conversation. They rarely allow you to speak as they unapologetically speak over others. Their arrogance and sense of superiority are obnoxious, and they believe only their ideas and opinions matter. To a narcissist, others' opinions and ideas appear flawed and inferior, regardless of how logical they are in reality.

3. They enjoy flattering and pleasing others and receiving the same in return.

Narcissists enjoy charming others and profiting from their admiration and praise. They flatter others to entice them and build a relationship with them. And why not? After all, others regard them as perfect and are constantly drawn to them. What is the logic? Some people may believe that associating with these narcissistic people will rub off on their "attractive" qualities.

4. Manipulation is one of their favorite techniques.

They use it to boost their perceived intelligence while making others feel inferior. They also manipulate others by playing the victim to make others feel guilty and give in to their demands.

A Narcissist Internal Conversation

Hey everyone! Look at me! Aren't I amazing? I'm the life of the party, and I know it. You all love me, don't you? I can tell by the way you're all looking at me.

I rule this party. It's my kingdom, and I'm the queen. Nobody else matters but me. And if you don't like it, well then, tough luck. I'll just ignore you until you come crawling back to me.

I'm the center of attention here, and I love it. Everybody wants a piece of me, and I'm more than happy to give it to them. But only on my terms. If you cross me, then you're done for.

I'm a king in my own world, and nobody can tell me what to do.

How To Know If You're in A Relationship with Someone With NPD?

1. Conversations are always focused on them.

The conversation is constantly redirected to their life and experiences. It could be about a past incident or a personal accomplishment. They frequently interrupt a story about you to draw attention back to themselves. If your point of view differs from theirs, they may correct, dismiss, or disregard you.

2. They thrive on compliments from you and others.

There is nothing wrong with receiving compliments; however, narcissists feed off the external validation they receive, which boosts their ego to such an extent that it validates their grandiose sense of self. If they constantly seek compliments from you or others when you are out in public, the narcissist is most likely looking for a supply of compliments.

3. They lack empathy and are unconcerned about your feelings.

When you need emotional support, narcissists appear cold and detached. They have difficulty making a genuine apology and accepting responsibility for any harm they cause.

4. They are very sensitive to criticism.

They react to constructive criticism with heated debates or abrupt detachment. A common reaction is judging, criticizing, or gaslighting you. They are also very skilled at holding you responsible for the problem or offense you brought to their attention.

What Does Narcissism Look Like at the Workplace and at Home?

How to Spot A Narcissist At the Workplace

Narcissism can sometimes be managed or avoided. Things become more difficult in professional settings. Working with a narcissistic coworker can be extremely frustrating. In the workplace, narcissism can be extremely toxic. Such people usually aspire to positions of leadership.

Common Characteristics of Narcissistic Coworkers.

1. They taking full credit for the team's success

When things go well, narcissists frequently take full responsibility for their success. They frequently undermine or minimize the participation of others.

Real-Life Experience:

I'm sure you know the type. They always have to be the center of attention and love taking credit for successes that they have nothing to do with. Well, I used to work with someone like that.

The sales team had been working hard to get a big client, and finally, we succeeded. But when the client came in, our narcissistic coworker, Jim*, took all the credit. He acted like he was the one who got us the client when in reality, he did nothing to help. In fact, he actually made it harder for us by telling everyone that we would never get the deal because we were not professional enough.

It was really frustrating because we all worked so hard on getting that client, and Jim just took all the credit without doing anything. Thankfully, Jim is no longer part of our team.

2. They avoiding accountability for mistakes made

While they are not afraid to take credit when things go well, narcissists rarely accept responsibility when problems arise. Instead, they blame others, lie about what happened, or downplay the gravity of the problem.

3. They are always demanding attention

Narcissists frequently appear self-centered and entitled. As a result, if they believe something is important, they may make a scene to draw attention to themselves.

4. They like gossiping about others

Narcissists thrive in chaos, and their triangulation tactics frequently pit coworkers or bosses against each other. They may spread rumors or gossip about others, especially if they are jealous or threatened by them.

5. They react negatively to constructive criticism

Narcissists frequently struggle with constructive feedback. They are extremely sensitive to criticism, and anything that threatens their ego may result in extreme defensiveness or anger as a reaction.

6. They're charismatic and convincing

Narcissists can appear charming and friendly. They may be well-liked by certain clients or colleagues, owing to their ability to make a good first impression.

7. They believe they are above the rules

When narcissists feel justified, they like to take shortcuts and make unethical decisions. They will, however, frequently hold others to a different standard.

8. They're extremely jealous

Despite their outward arrogance, narcissists often feel profoundly empty and insecure. They are prone to becoming envious at the slightest hint of someone else's good fortune.

A Narcissist Boss

A narcissistic boss requires constant praise and is frequently volatile. The key to dealing with such a boss is maintaining your perspective on your responsibilities regardless of their reactions. Failure to do so can be detrimental to your mental and emotional health.

Common characteristics of a Narcissistic Boss.

1. They almost exclusively talk about themselves.

Bosses with narcissistic personality disorder are constantly thinking about themselves. They are conscious of physical appearance, wealth, talents, and accomplishments and expect your full attention while telling you about them. These comments may be exaggerated and are not always true reflections of their lives.

2. They require constant praise.

Despite their outward confidence, narcissists are often quite vulnerable and insecure, with fragile self-esteem. They require near-constant attention, praise, and admiration to keep themselves going. They may also expect to be recognized as superior despite doing nothing worthy of praise.

3. They take advantage of others.

Many people are naturally drawn to narcissists because they can appear attractive, charismatic, and charming. As a result, narcissists may have no trouble getting people to do what they want, even if it means causing work burnout for those who work for them. They get bored easily and seek constant entertainment wherever they can find it.

4. They lack empathy.

Narcissists cannot empathize with others or recognize that others may be experiencing their own difficulties. Even if they recognize other people's difficulties, they don't understand why these people don't change to meet their own.

Real-Life Story:

When Jerry*, the boss discovered that the workers had made a mistake with the client's order, he was furious. He yelled and screamed at them, calling them incompetent and useless. The workers tried to explain what happened, but Jerry would not hear of it. He just kept berating them until they were in tears. Finally, he sent them all home for the day, humiliated and defeated.

5. They are irritated by criticism.

Narcissists are extremely sensitive to criticism because of their fragile egos. Any remarks that draw attention to their insecurities or flaws may be met with a fit of narcissistic rage.

How to Spot A Narcissist at Home

A Narcissist Child

A child's inability to develop emotional and relational awareness may indicate that they are developing narcissistic personality disorder (NPD). A lack of empathy, an unrealistic sense of self-importance, a lack of recognition of attention and admiration, and an overall struggle in social and family relationships are all signs that a child may be a narcissist. How can you tell if you have a narcissistic child?

Signs your Child could be Narcissistic.

1. They have difficulties making and keeping friends.

Children with NPD struggle in all relationships, but it will be especially noticeable in peer relationships. While most children sort through their peers until they find good-fitting connections, children with NPD rarely "settle into" lasting friendships because they lack empathy, the ability to take responsibility, and a strong sense of envy.

2. They put other kids down.

Narcissistic children don't understand why being critical and mean to other children or talking about other children to adults is problematic. This criticism is true in the child's mind, and hearing adults speak positively about other children is painful to them.

3. They blame others for their mistakes.

Since they believe adults are untrustworthy and incompetent, children with NPD develop grandiose or withdrawn attitudes as a protective defense mechanism. As a result, a child with NPD will blame all of their wrongdoing and mishaps on the adults or children around them.

4. Consistent haughty behavior.

Children with NPD have an internalized belief that they are different from others. Externally, this can appear as the child being indifferent to attempts to engage and connect. They can be dismissive and even comment on others' inferiority.

5. Inability to accept and take responsibility.

Children with narcissism believe they are unique and their needs come first. They frequently refuse to admit when they are mistaken because they cannot comprehend how this could be. They were acting to meet their own needs, in their minds.

Real Life Story

Even as a young child, Nathan was always very self-centered. When playing with other kids in school, he would always be the one to take charge, bossing everyone around and demanding that they do things his way. If someone didn't want to play by his rules, Nathan would quickly become frustrated and angry, often yelling and throwing tantrums.

Things were no different at home, either. Nathan was always the one who wanted to be in control of everything, whether it was playing with his siblings or watching TV. Nathan would get angry and resort to bullying tactics if anyone dared to disagree with him or didn't want to do what he wanted. His siblings soon learned that it was best not to cross him if they wanted peace in the house.

A Narcissist Husband.

It's no secret that narcissism can be difficult in relationships. You've most likely heard someone lament their life with a narcissistic husband. They likely discuss cheating, self-centeredness, or other behaviors that make life more difficult to manage with that narcissistic spouse. Having a spouse who loves excessive admiration and is willing to take advantage of others is challenging. Here's how to spot a Narcissistic husband.

Real-life Story

John* was a wealthy man who cared about one thing and one thing only - his appearance. He would spend hours in front of the mirror each day, ensuring every hair was in place, and his clothes were perfectly tailored. He never gave much thought to his wife, Liz*, or their children, who were often sickly because he refused to buy quality nutritious food for them. Instead, he spent all of his money on designer clothes and accessories.

Liz and the children suffered as a result of John's vanity. She was often left alone at home while he went out drinking with his friends. The children rarely saw him because he was always too busy working. They were also dirty and underfed, but John didn't care. All that mattered to him was how he looked at others.

One day, John's greed got the best of him. He had been caught up in a financial scandal and had lost all of his money. His family was forced to move away from their luxurious lifestyle into a small apartment in the city. They were surrounded by families who were just scraping by and could no longer afford to buy nice clothes or eat well. John was humiliated and angry at himself for being so foolish. His attitude changed overnight once they were living in poverty, and he blamed Liz and children for his misfortune. He said they were ungrateful for everything he had done for them.

John also became abusive towards them, yelling at them constantly for no reason. The only time he seemed happy was when he was beating them or insulting them publicly. Finally, after years of abuse, Liz had enough and left him with the kids. John never saw them again - nor did he ever care to find out about their wellbeing.

Signs of a Narcissistic husband

1. There is little to no empathy.

Narcissists are so preoccupied with their own needs and feelings that they frequently fail to empathize with others. It means that if you have a narcissistic husband, he will frequently disregard your feelings. He may insult you, annoy you, or engage in selfish behavior without considering how it affects you.

2. They like accusing others

Narcissistic husbands may not accept any wrongdoing because of their fragile self-esteem. They will almost certainly blame you for your bad behavior if they do. For example, if your narcissistic husband has an affair, he will most likely blame you and claim that you drove him to do it due to some flaw in your character or behavior.

3. Excessive sensitivity to criticism

Nobody wants to hear that they've done something wrong or fallen short of expectations, but narcissists can't handle negative feedback. If you even imply that your narcissistic husband should do something different, he will become enraged. If you offer constructive criticism, he may begin verbally insulting you or go so far as to break household objects.

4. Constantly about himself

Narcissists, in addition to bragging, frequently talk about themselves. If you try to talk about something else, your husband may dominate the conversation, give you little opportunity to speak or shift the subject back to himself. You might even notice that when the two of you sit down to dinner, he spends the entire time telling you about his day and never asks how yours went.

5. Obsession with outward appearances

Since narcissists want the best of everything, they will spend a lot of time and effort on their physical appearance. This entails spending hours at the gym, buying expensive colognes and cosmetics, and insisting on the most expensive clothing. Because your husband puts so much effort into his appearance and only associates with those people he considers special, he will most likely expect you to look your best at all times. He may insist on you going on diets, getting your hair done, or even having plastic surgery to maintain your outward beauty because you are associated with him.

Final Takeaway

As you can see, narcissism is a spectrum disorder that can manifest in different ways. It's critical to know the signs and symptoms of NPD so that you can protect yourself and you deal with them effectively. There are many resources available to you, and by understanding and recognizing narcissistic personality disorder, you can start taking steps towards healthier relationships.

The next chapter will discuss the question of if a Narcissistic relationship is toxic. Let's find out more of what this relationship is and can be.

Chapter 2: Is A Relationship with A Narcissist a Toxic Relationship?

No one enters into a relationship with the intention of it being toxic, but sometimes that is exactly what happens. In a toxic relationship, you either feel unloved, unappreciated or threatened. Simply put, a toxic relationship consistently drains your energy rather than replenishing it. It is toxic when your mental, emotional, or physical health is jeopardized due to that relationship. Being in a relationship with a narcissist can be extremely damaging, and it is important to know if you are in one. In this chapter, we will explore the signs that you may be in a toxic relationship with one.

Signs of a Toxic Relationship

At Work

Toxic work relationships can take many forms in the workplace. It can happen when one or more people consistently leave you feeling emotionally unsupported, misunderstood, or undermined. It's not uncommon to experience workplace bullying or a lack of support from coworkers. Some warning indicators of a toxic work relationship are;

1. **Gaslighting**

One key narcissistic behavior is gaslighting. This happens when the person feeds you a false narrative and convinces you that you are at fault. Although the word "gaslighting" is more commonly applied to interpersonal relationships, it can also occur in the workplace when a coworker or boss manipulates you into doubting your sanity or the integrity of your observations. They'll try to pin it on you. It's a more subtle form than overt harassment when occurring.

2. **If your Manager/ Boss demands too much of your time.**

Do you frequently stay on the phone, work late, or complete tasks for your superiors or peers when you're not officially on the clock? When a coworker constantly demands too much of your time and then takes credit for your efforts, it may be time to reevaluate your working relationship with them.

3. **If there is Abuse of power**

If you don't want to do something, your boss will use their authority to force you to. A senior manager or employee may try to shift your responsibility for tasks. Be on the watch out for senior staff members who treat you poorly, make you uncomfortable, or otherwise negatively impact your mental health since they may be engaging in some form of power abuse.

4. **It's getting too personal.**

There's a logic behind the common desire to maintain the boundary between one's private and professional lives. When a colleague at work becomes too close to you, it might harm your professional development. Getting too close, especially with a boss who likes to gossip about other employees is not a good thing and needs to be stopped.

Toxic Relationships in the Family

This is what a toxic relationship looks like in the family.

1. **They are Abusive**

Initial indicators of a toxic person or setting include any form of physical, mental, or emotional abuse. Toxic behavior includes using words to put down a member of the family. Regardless of who the aggression is aimed towards, a display of emotionally damaging words or physical force is wrong and should raise serious red flags.

Real-life Story:

Christina Crawford _portrays her adoptive mother, Joan Crawford as a narcissist in her book, Mommie Dearest. She indicates how she was physically abused on several occasions and how her mother put more importance on her acting career rather than parenting._

2. **You are always the target of their criticism and blame.**

A toxic relative is someone quick to criticize or place blame on others but slow to accept responsibility for their actions. They may blame others for everything, insist that their problems are always your fault, or otherwise do whatever they can to avoid taking any responsibility for their actions.

3. **They have a manipulative personality**.

Toxic people are almost always manipulative, and their tactics can take many forms. They may try to manipulate you by using techniques like gaslighting and guilt-tripping. Someone is toxic in the family if they manipulate you or make you feel guilty or awful when you don't do what they want you to do.

4. **They are highly competitive**

Sibling rivalry is an outcome of toxic family dynamics. The impact of perfectionism on children and the effects of sibling comparison on children's sense of self-worth can be devastating.

5. They exert control

Another hallmark of a dysfunctional family unit is dominating behavior, most often exhibited by a parent but also conceivable among siblings. It might manifest as little regard for another person's decisions, impossible expectations, and conditional affection.

6. Being in their presence makes you feel anxious or nervous.

A toxic relative or home environment might also be identified by the way you feel when you're there. Mood swings, anxiety, low self-esteem, and a constant sense of being on edge are some of the emotions that may be present. How you feel when you're around your family or thinking about spending time with them is the most telling indicator that your family dynamic is unhealthy.

Toxic Relationship with a Spouse or Friend

Here's how to spot a toxic relationship in your personal life.

1. There is toxic communication

Married but in a toxic relationship often have trouble communicating with one another. Some partners in a relationship pick fights over nothing, are constantly critical of one another, or use sarcasm as a shield against their true sentiments. Some people may stop interacting with one another. In the long term, mediocre communication inside a marriage is no better than no communication. A couple having trouble communicating could indicate toxicity in the relationship. Trust, emotional intimacy and affection cannot exist in a relationship where one partner refuses to listen to the other. If one partner leaves the room while the other is talking, avoids, or becomes angry, it may indicate a communication breakdown.

2. **They are controlling**

Manipulation, passive-aggression, and verbal abuse are all methods of behavioral control. The controlling partner may resort to physical violence if they believe they are losing power or want to intimidate their partner into submission. The marriage will be extremely toxic if this is the case.

Controlling behavior in finances is a telltale symptom of a controlling relationship. If one partner is hiding money or spending too much, that might cause financial difficulties, and confronting that partner about it is not controlling. When one partner has complete financial control over the other and either refuses to share or criticizes the other partner for meeting their fundamental requirements, this is not a healthy relationship.

Real-life Story:

Duante* demanded constant attention and praise and would get angry if he didn't get it. Soon, my work life was consumed by his needs. He would call or text me constantly during the day, wanting to know what I was doing and where I was. If I didn't respond right away, he would get angry and start berating me.

3. **They are insensitive to your needs and emotions**

It's painful when your lover doesn't take your feelings seriously. It's a solid sign that your marriage is toxic if you and your partner both indulge in this behavior. Disrespect in a marriage shows up in different ways. Lack of support, envy, harsh comments, reluctance to interact, and resentment are all possible responses to being disrespected. Couples sometimes disrespect one another by using derogatory language or making threats. The connection may be disrespectful overall if they ignore you.

4. There is lack of support

How can you tell if your spouse is not supportive of you? The correct response is, "it depends." The absence of help can take various forms. Sometimes a spouse can give the impression that they don't care when you're telling them something significant about yourself, like the events of your day.

For example, if you both have kids, the problem could be that you spend all your free time caring for them while your partner does nothing. You may also believe your partner does not appreciate you even though you do most of the work in the relationship. The key indicators of a dysfunctional marriage are feelings of isolation and lack of support.

5. There is deep resentment in the relationship

Any feelings of blame or guilt that arise as a result of resentment are usually directed at the other spouse. If neither of you is willing to talk about what's going wrong in the relationship, pointing fingers won't help. If both partners in a toxic marriage can keep their cool and be civil when confronting each other about the relationship's flaws, that will be a huge start in the right direction toward mending the bonds.

The anger that results from marital frustration and resentment is understandable and undesirable. If one partner in a marriage feels underappreciated and unwanted, resentment might develop. Anger and resentment on the part of one partner can damage a marriage by dampening feelings of intimacy and commitment between the two partners. It's advised that partners not go to bed upset at each other.

6. Pressure all the time

Every married couple goes through stressful times, and unhappiness in a marriage is often a precursor to overall stress. When tensions never seem to wane, it signifies a troubled marriage. It's not easy to juggle a full schedule between working, paying bills, raising kids, maintaining a clean and well-stocked home, making repairs, going to restaurants, and having fun. These obligations and the pressures they place on us can easily build up to the point of stress. Frustration and rage can result when spouses sharply disagree over these tasks and duties.

Real Life Story:

Suzanna Quintana, an Abusive Recovery Coach, says that living with a narcissist means living in perpetual confusion. She says that Living with a narcissistic individual can be an incredibly frustrating and disorienting experience. These individuals often seem like the perfect partner or spouse on the outside, projecting an image of flawlessness and projecting unrealistic expectations onto their loved ones. However, behind closed doors, things are quite different. With a narcissist, the reality is constantly being distorted and manipulated to fit their own agenda and interests, leaving those living with them constantly feeling off-balance and uncertain.

Constant fear and insecurity become the norm, as you never know exactly what to expect from your partner or how they will react to even the most basic of requests or needs. Whether sleeping, eating, or simply existing in his presence, you find yourself walking on eggshells at all times, never knowing when you will set him off or provoke his wrath. In short, living with a narcissist is an experience that is both exhausting and maddening - one that I wouldn't wish on anyone.

Takeaway

With a narcissist, it's hard to see the signs that you're in a toxic relationship. The abuse can be subtle and insidious, creeping up on you over time until you feel like you're walking on eggshells all the time. It's important to understand what to look for so that you can take steps to protect yourself and get out of the relationship if necessary. The signs we've outlined here are a starting point; if you have any concerns about your relationship, please reach out for help. There is no shame in admitting that you need support — in fact, it takes courage. Our next chapter will introduce you to the consequences of these relationships.

Chapter 3: The Consequences of Staying in A Toxic Relationship

Is your current romantic relationship unhealthy? How can you identify signs of a toxic relationship? How do you move past the point where you are unsure what to do next and take the necessary actions to restore your emotional health? Understanding the long-term effects of toxic relationships, spotting the signs, and getting the support you need to end a bad friendship are crucial. Yes, it's perfectly ok to want your relationship to be more stable and compatible. However, you might need to alter the dynamics of your interaction within it. All or any of the parties involved can make this happen by putting in a therapeutic effort.

Whether an abusive, lying, cheating husband or a treacherous ex-girlfriend from your youth, they've both served as roadblocks to your success. Or a coworker who plays nice when they need your help but isn't above using you as a pawn in the corporate chess game. How have these people affected your life and those of your children (if in a marriage with children)? Let's find out!

The Effects of a Toxic Family or Home
Consequences of a toxic relationship in the family (to children)

Some parents believe that staying in a bad marriage is for the best of their children because everyone wants what's best for their kids. However, it's undeniable that the family and upbringing shape who you are as a person, even though psychologists argue over which influences personality and behavior more strongly: nature or nurture.

As discussed below, staying in a toxic relationship may affect you/ your children in these ways.

1. **You loose concept of who you are.**

Your childhood experiences can have long-lasting effects on your character. You might have never found your true identity if your upbringing was unstable or inconsistent. This is especially true if you were raised to be selfless and are constantly expected to help out regardless of your situation. Having a strong sense of identity is difficult for many people because of their experiences growing up in a dysfunctional family. To blend in, you may feel like you've taken on some or all of the characteristics of the people around you, or you may feel like you've completely transformed into a new person every day. Growing up in a dysfunctional household is often accompanied by an unstable sense of self, which can cause various emotional and mental health problems.

2. **Children become distant and unapproachable to all those around them.**

If you were brought up in a toxic family with emotionally distant members, you might have difficulty building intimate and close relationships. A child's dread of having a relationship like the one they saw between their parents can be traced back to the fact that they regard their parents as a model of love. Trusting others and forming strong bonds may be challenging for them.

If you were never taught to be vulnerable as a child, it could be difficult to open up to others. It's understandable if sharing your emotions causes extreme distress; protecting yourself from potential harm may lead you to avoid doing so.

3. **Children are constantly walking on eggshells.**

Many dysfunctional families are characterized by extreme swings in their members' emotional states. Uncontrollable parents with rage issues or other mental health problems make the home very unstable. This is from growing up with these kinds of responses from loved ones would leave you with a crippling fear of upsetting them. If you're used to seeing strong reactions to conflict, you might be reluctant to correct or confront someone if they upset you because of your history with anger or violence.

4. They seek out a toxic relationship.

One of the telltale signs of having come from a dysfunctional family is a propensity toward or persistence in unhealthy romantic relationships. Some people take a lifetime to realize they have this problem, despite this being the most challenging and harmful trait that toxic family members can instill in you. We actively pursue the kind of love we've been conditioned to expect. You set an excellent example as a parent. Children who grow up in dysfunctional homes may copy their parents' marital patterns. If your children constantly witness you arguing, they may grow up to believe that such behavior is socially acceptable. If you were raised in an extremely overprotective environment and never allowed to live a "normal" childhood, you might attract a possessive, possessive, or controlling partner. Although these types of relationships are often fraught with hurt and heartbreak, the familiarity of the pattern can be a source of strange comfort. This is because children will not be able to differentiate between a regular and dysfunctional relationship.

5. They constantly consider themselves at fault

Unmanaged parents' anger can lead them to blame everyone but themselves for their children's difficulties. So often, it's the kids who end up taking the blame. It's possible that you were raised to blame yourself for everything in your dysfunctional family. You can always find a way to blame yourself, even when you have done nothing to deserve it.

6. **They become perfectionists**

Difficulty accepting failure is a common trait among people who grew up with excessively strict and demanding parents. If you were raised believing you could never measure up, you might still struggle with perfectionism as an adult. Experiencing setbacks is inevitable, and they often present invaluable learning opportunities. It's not simple to shrug off setbacks when you've been taught that failure means you're weak or unworthy.

7. **It's hard for you to recall your younger years.**

Why you don't remember certain things or have a hazy childhood memory may be complex. The effects of stress and trauma on memory are not always clear. This may be your brain's way of coping with the toxicity of your upbringing, especially if you have large gaps in your memory or would rather not think about your childhood.

8. **After spending time with your loved ones, you feel completely drained.**

The effects of a toxic family can linger long after you've left home. There may be unhealthy dynamics at play if talking to family members always leaves you feeling mentally or emotionally drained. Your loved ones are supposed to be there for you and comfort you. However, visiting them may feel more like a burden than a reward if you grew up with abusive parents.

9. **Children develop behavioral issues.**

Children raised in toxic homes are more likely to have emotional difficulties than adults. children will develop unhealthy coping mechanisms to deal with their feelings. Habits like compulsive video game playing or comfort eating are picked up to adjust to the pressure they feel at home. They may also start displaying their feelings in different contexts. They may start acting out violently or radically change their academic performance. Depression and other mood disorders are among the many causes of such problematic behavior. If left untreated, these difficulties might snowball into substance abuse. In some cases, children develop fears and phobias, which make their adult life more complicated. If these problems are not treated before they become more entrenched, they may persist throughout adulthood.

Real-Life Story:

Amina's children knew that their home was a scary, unpredictable place. Their dad, Ahmed* could fly into a rage for no reason, and would often use verbal abuse and threats to control them. He would also constantly put them down, telling them they were worthless and would never amount to anything.

The result of living with such a volatile father was that both of Amina's kids developed low self-esteem and substance abuse problems as teenagers. They both struggled in school and had difficulty making friends. It was only after they both left home and started getting help for their issues that they began to understand how much damage their narcistic dad had done.

Consequences of Staying in a Toxic Work Relationship

1. Mood Disorders

Depression is one of the top three issues that workers face in the workplace. Most of the time, workers are blissfully unaware of their predicament. A toxic work environment may discourage them from seeking help even if they know the problem. Sadness, disinterest, irritability, headaches, difficulty concentrating, guilt, and other negative emotions may significantly impact workers' health. Because of the culture of fear in the workplace, many workers are too afraid to seek help.

2. Stress and worry

Constant worry about going to work can cause a lot of unnecessary stress. Physical anxiety symptoms, such as restlessness, irritability, and a rapid heart rate, can make it difficult for employees to focus on their work. Avoiding work, having negative thoughts and reactions, and being unable to get things done are all consequences of anxiety. The paranoia that often accompanies anxiety only worsens things in a hostile work environment.

3. It can cause extreme anxiety

There is more than just psychological damage associated with stress. It can cause changes in brain structure, post-traumatic stress disorder, impaired immune function, and an increased risk of depression. The employee's performance suffers from stress, trapping them in a position where they cannot ask for assistance.

4. **It makes you feel tired**

Tired all the time? Indeed, that's typical of a hostile work environment. Working under such stress can take a mental toll, resulting in a lack of sleep or even insomnia. A person with chronic fatigue may experience a loss of libido, social withdrawal, digestive problems, and even migraines. Constant fatigue is a risk factor for burnout and job loss.

5. **It can cause sickness**

Many employees report becoming physically ill more frequently while working in an intimidating or hostile environment. When you add stress and fatigue, your immune system weakens, and you're more likely to get sick. You may experience muscle soreness, a cold-like state, or the development of ulcers due to your stomach's increased acid production. If an employee's physical health is suffering, they are more likely to call out sick, adding stress to the situation. Many occupational exposures have the same negative impact on self-reported physical health and mental health as second-hand smoke. Stress lowers the immune system, which makes you sick.

Having low-quality relationships can make you feel guilty and unworthy. Depressive symptoms are exacerbated in toxic work settings. There is more at play than just physical harm. A lack of job security, an unbalanced work-life, and a lack of control result from working in a toxic workplace. Overeating, excessive alcohol consumption, and tobacco use are just a few negative health habits that can develop.

Consequences of Staying in a Toxic Friendship

1. **You develop a poor opinion of oneself**

If you have a toxic friend, spending time with them is likely to make you feel worse about yourself than if you didn't spend time with them. Hearing a friend constantly be negative and question your abilities or point out your flaws can cause you to doubt yourself. A vicious cycle of low self-esteem, complacency in the friendship, and resistance to ending it can result.

2. **Your stress levels increase around that person**

Spending time with a friend who constantly complains about other people and feels the need to play the victim can be exhausting and depressing. A person who is always talking about themselves can also be very distracting. Good friends are meant to be supportive of each other. This relationship can be constantly bombarded with drama and rumors which is not good for your sanity.

3. **It drains you of loving yourself and others.**

Knowing you're in a toxic friendship can be challenging, especially if you've invested time and energy into the relationship. Knowing that you've put so much effort into a friendship that has yielded so little in return (and probably caused you a great deal of frustration) can be disheartening. But examine how your feelings about this friendship truly stand. Whether or not it makes you feel bad about yourself and your life is something you will notice. Anyone with a good friend knows they are an invaluable resource for coping with life's challenges and protecting their emotional well-being. However, the opposite is also true. This toxic relationship can discourage you from making true good friends because it takes so much from you.

Consequences of Staying in a Toxic Romantic Relationship

The marital relationship is challenging and with a narcissist partner its double the effort. Many people marry a narcissist with the hope of changing them in marriage. However, this never works and they suffer greatly in a romantic marital relationship. These are the consequences of being in a marital relationship with a narcissist.

1. **You are always anxious**

The majority of people who have overcome narcissistic abuse experience anxiety. It's common for victims of narcissistic abuse to be terrified of forming new friendships or romantic partnerships. In the relationship, you are always anxious of how the person will behave and you are almost always walking on eggshells and being unsure of yourself with constant gaslighting.

Real-life Story:

Joanne* was married to Joe* for 5 years, and she could not stand it anymore. Every day was a battle and Joanne never knew what mood he's be in. One minute Joe was sweet and loving; the next minute, he was screaming at her for no reason. Joanne was tired of walking on eggshells all the time.

2. **You feel depressed**

Many victims of narcissistic abuse also struggle with clinical depression. After being verbally abused where they were told that they are useless and stupid by their abuser, survivors often struggle with feelings of worthlessness. After being controlled and gaslighted for so long, you may also withdraw from others, which might amplify your existing sentiments of despair and cause deep depression.

3. You may experience Post-Traumatic Stress Disorder (PTSD)

PTSD symptoms are common among people who have survived narcissistic abuse. You'll be on the lookout for any threats as your mind goes into high-alert mode. This is because your body is prepared for battle or flight in response to stressful occurrences. Therefore, anything connected to those recollections can set off an anxiety attack.

If you've suffered narcissistic abuse, you're always feel on edge. Many people who a narcissist has abused have said they could never predict their abuser's behavior. It can be difficult to unwind if you're constantly on guard for your abuser and waiting for them to appear around every corner. You might also try to avoid anything that brings up unpleasant memories of the abuse. This can include avoiding specific locations or persons.

4. Feeling of Worthlessness

You may feel as if you have entirely lost yourself. Narcissistic abuse is a sort of indoctrination that can ruin your sense of self-worth. You could not recognize yourself as the same person you were before you got into a controlling relationship. Those who have suffered narcissistic abuse often have trouble recognizing their reflection because they no longer see their true self reflected. You might also have trouble trusting themselves, or even the people closest to you, because they are plagued with self-doubt and second-guessing. The victim of abuse may start to doubt their worth or assume they are to blame for the attacks. Feelings of humiliation and shame may prevent you from seeking assistance. Making choices could be difficult for you as well.

5. **Unable to Forgive Oneself**

Many survivors of narcissistic abuse suffer from feelings of worthlessness or the conviction that they deserve the narcissist's treatment. If someone you thought loved you unconditionally exploited their power to hurt you, it's natural to question whether there's something fundamentally wrong with you. Your narcissistic abuser's poor treatment of you may have contributed to low self-esteem and the belief that you could have done more to deserve better treatment.

6. **Physical and Cognitive Problems**

Physical symptoms, such as migraines, stomachaches, and bodily pains, may persist after victims of narcissistic abuse finally get help. Narcissistic abuse can cause a variety of symptoms, including insomnia. The day's events may have left you feeling anxious, making it hard for you to relax and drift off to sleep. Otherwise, you might experience persistent nightmares for days. After experiencing narcissistic abuse, it's possible that you'll find it challenging to focus on even the most routine activities, such as doing a project at work or watching television. It's well knowledge that recalling painful experiences can make it difficult to pay attention. Short-term memory loss is a possibility.

7. **You have trust problems**

Trust issues are common after surviving narcissistic abuse. This may appear beneficial at first, but it may end up being detrimental to your romantic prospects in the long run. Issues like social anxiety could be a fallout of this problem. You may always be questioning whether or not the people in your life are being honest with you or are just using your emotions to obtain what they want. Fear of being betrayed may cause you to become hypervigilant and too sensitive to the opinions of others. Trust problems can affect your life, from romantic partnerships to friendships to professional connections and even interactions with close relatives. And if you suffer from insecure attachment, you may have a persistent fear that the people you care about may abandon or betray you.

8. **You become a people pleaser**

You could develop a desire to gain the approval of others and give in to this tendency. Due to the long period spent tiptoeing around people's expectations, you may become overly accommodating to gain their favor. After experiencing narcissistic abuse, you may have difficulty putting your feelings and thoughts into words because of what others think of you. When dealing with a narcissist, it's best to keep emotions at bay to avoid an uncomfortable confrontation.

9. **You are prone to addictions that can destroy your life**

Narcissist abuse can also lead to damaging behaviors. Those in a controlling relationship may blame themselves for their partner's abusive conduct, leading them to punish themselves. You could have dependency issues with alcohol, tobacco, food, or money. Addictions like these may be used to avoid feeling uncomfortable emotions.

10. You may have destroyed your life in the relationship

When it comes to narcissists, the damage they can cause to your life can seem impossible. They have a way of jeopardizing your career and taking away your self-esteem, leaving you feeling hopeless and disheartened. In many cases, the sole purpose of their destructive behavior is to ruin you completely and utterly.

Real-life Story:

My name is Ava* and I used to be a successful career woman. I had a great job and was always on top of my game. But then I met Charlie, a narcissist who ruined it all.

Charlie was charming and manipulative, and he convinced me to do things that weren't in my best interests; he convinced me to quit my job and move away from my family and friends. And worst of all, Charlie convinced me to give up my self-respect. Eventually, I realized what he was doing to me, but it was too late. My career was gone, and I could blame no one else but myself.

11. Experience an alteration of appetite

As a result of their mental and physical health problems, many people lose their appetite. They aren't hungry because of the stress and this can lead to an increase in eating disorders and other ailments. There is a lack of strength because the body isn't getting enough food and vitamins. There are also cases where people start eating excessively in the same way they find solace in eating. Since many people, especially women, suffer from low self-esteem, unhealthy diets are often used to achieve a thinner body.

12. They shut off all communication with the outside

When people are in an unhealthy relationship, people tend to isolate themselves. They avoid social interaction as much as possible in their daily lives. As a result of feeling used and manipulated, they struggle with anger. Consequently, they worry that everyone is always finding fault with them.

13. They may have suicidal thoughts

The frequency with which people entertain suicidal thoughts increases when they are in an unhealthy relationship. Suicide becomes an attractive option for those in toxic relationships because of the feeling of not having any other choice but to end their own lives rather than continue to suffer. In their professional lives, many psychologists have also come across similar situations.

14. They feel suffocated and helpless

Some people feel like they are suffocating in an unhealthy relationship because they are afraid to express their emotions to their partners. In addition, they experience a sense of helplessness because they cannot do anything to improve the situation.

There are a lot of unhealthy relationships out there, and they usually end up affecting everyone involved. Phoenix Rising Coaching's break-up coach, Von Fisher, talks about how the experience of having a partner who repeatedly criticized her and others for his failures motivated her to start her new business as a breakup/divorce coach.

Real-life Story:

I'm Emma* and I was in a relationship with a narcissist for two years. It was the worst experience of my life. Bryan* would constantly put me down, make me feel like I was *nothing. Worst of all he'd cheat on me. The thing is, I couldn't leave him. I was obsessed with him. Bryan had this way of making me think that I needed him and no one else could ever love me like he did. It was a sick, twisted dynamic that I couldn't escape from.*

15. They Lose self-confidence

If you're in a toxic relationship, you probably feel less confident than you otherwise would since they blame themselves whenever anything goes wrong, or a dispute arises. They begin to suspect personal flaws, which leads to a steady erosion of self-assurance. Many people also begin to have doubts about their abilities and decisions. Some people even begin to harm themselves physically. They have low self-esteem because they are critical of being overweight, black, short, bald, etc. They are constantly critical of themselves and feel unworthy of love.

16. They experience depression and other mental illnesses

Some victims may develop mental illnesses and require ongoing therapy to function normally. Unfortunately, this can also cause sleep issues for some people. Many people experience mental health issues like breakdowns, low self-worth, helplessness, fear, anxiety, depression, paranoia, and even narcissism as a direct result of an unhealthy relationship. In her BTR podcast, Anne Blythe interviews Diane, who expresses how a narcissistic husband made her depressed. She explains how she felt inadequate and exhausted by the whole situation. This had a serious impact on her mental health.

Final Takeaway

So, is a relationship with a narcissist a toxic relationship? The answer is most definitely yes! If you are in contact with or have relationship with someone who displays any of the signs of toxicity we've mentioned, it's time to re-think the relationship. The effects of living with or being around a narcissist can be devastating and long-lasting, especially for children. In the next chapter, we discuss the biggest effect, depression.

·

Chapter 4: Dealing with Depression As A result of Being In A Narcissistic Relationship

Narcissists are experts at deception and manipulation. You have probably experienced or witnessed some of the narcissist's destructive conduct if you have encountered one in your life. Narcissistic abuse frequently begins subtly and then escalates.

Forms of Narcissistic Abuse

1. Emotional - Talking down to, manipulative tactics, such as ignoring you, isolating you, lying are common in narcissistic relationships.
2. Mental- Accusations, criticism, gaslighting and threats are common in narcissistic relationships.
3. Physical – physical violence may be part of the abuse.
4. Financial – control and withholding money in the home is very common
5. Sexual abuse- may include rape.

Narcissistic Abuse Syndrome (NAS)

This is a collection of symptoms experienced by victims of narcissistic abuse comparable to those of post-traumatic stress disorder. Some symptoms include:

1. Being constantly on guard
2.Having intrusive, invasive, or unwanted thoughts; having flashbacks;
3. Fear by avoiding triggers
4. Feeling lonely and distressed;
5. Denial of reality and avoiding situations that may trigger these feelings.

All these symptoms are caused by the behaviour patterns of the Narcissist described above and can lead to depression. Unfortunately, depression is a common reaction to being in a relationship with a narcissist. Here are the ways to identify and deal with depression caused by a narcissistic partner.

Signs and Symptoms of Depression Caused by A Narcissistic Partner

How Narcissists Create a Sense of Loneliness that Causes Depression

In many cases, narcissists use isolation and loneliness as a way to abuse their victims. Typically, they will actively isolate their victims from friends and family, weakening their support network and leaving them more vulnerable to the narcissist's manipulation and exploitation. Additionally, by creating a sense of loneliness within their victims, the narcissist is able to take advantage of emotional needs that may have been left unfulfilled due to past experiences or childhood trauma. By keeping the victim trapped in an emotional limbo between hope and despair, the narcissist maintains power and control over them. Ultimately, what starts as emotional abuse can quickly evolve into other forms of neglect or worse if left unchecked. Therefore, recognizing patterns of isolation and loneliness in relationships with narcissistic partners is critical for both mental and physical safety. This is also a big cause of depression because there is no support to share the experiences.

Signs of Depression

1. You feel helpless and frozen

When dealing with a narcissistic relationship, one of the most common signs and symptoms of depression can be feeling frozen in place. If you feel unable to fight back against the abusive behaviors of your partner or if you simply cannot run away, you may find yourself experiencing feelings of apathy or inaction. Alternatively, some people may resort to fawning or trying to please their partner as a way of managing their emotions.

2. You struggle with indecision.

Low self-worth and confidence are common results of repeated instances of being put down or criticized. Constant suggestions that you are a lousy person who can't seem to do anything right are a common kind of narcissistic manipulation. For example, an abusive partner may use deceptively friendly language to tell you that you're foolish or uninformed, such as *"Honey, you're so dumb. Without me, how would you get by?"*

You can begin to internalize the criticism and let it color your view of yourself, leading to persistent self-doubt. You may start to question your judgment if someone is gaslighting you. If you're led to believe by deception that certain events didn't occur, you may start to question your sanity. Because of this emotional and mental abuse, it may be difficult to make choices in the future.

3. Feeling that you did something wrong.

One of the hallmarks of narcissism is an inability to accept blame for one's mistakes or destructive behaviors. Abusive spouses will often try to shift the blame for their behavior onto you, making you feel guilty.

Real-Life Story:

Peter* was a narcissist. He always thought he was better than everyone else and that he could do no wrong. So, when his wife, Esther*, caught him cheating on her, she was not surprised. In fact, she had been expecting it for a while.

What Esther didn't expect, however, was the way Peter turned the blame on her. He said that she was useless and unattractive to him and that was the reason he went to sleep with another woman. Esther couldn't believe her ears! She had been there for him through thick and thin, but he repaid her by cheating on her?

She decided it was time to leave Peter. She packed her bags and walked out of their home, never to look back.

4. **Unexplained Physical Symptoms**

Anxiety and nervousness are common responses to abuse and may manifest themselves physically.

Perhaps you've noticed:

- Changes in your appetite
- Nausea and/or stomach distress
- Gastrointestinal issues such as discomfort and nausea
- Pain and discomfort in the muscles
- Insomnia or difficulty to sleep
- Fatigue and lethargy
- Alcohol and drug abuse

The alcohol and drug abuse happens gradually to cope with unpleasant emotions or physical pain of being in the narcissistic relationship.

Real-Life Story from the founder of the Amazing Me Movement, Iva Ursano;

"When I began dating my narcissistic boyfriend, I realized many red flags that I should have looked out for. However, my self-love and self-esteem were low then, and I did not consider the red flags and held on to him, hoping that things would get better and he would grow to love me again and change his behaviors. Unfortunately, that did not happen. After a couple of years, the emotional and verbal abuse got worse. Sometimes he would say he was sorry, and often he made me believe that everything was my fault and that if I only listened to him and did what he said, we would live in peace.

I kept holding on hope, but at some point, the bullying and the verbal abuses were so bad that they landed me in the hospital with so much back pain.

Later, I discovered that this pain in my back resulted from the hatred and anger I was carrying for him.

After staying with him for eight years, I was emotionally drained and had nothing left inside me, so I finally walked out bearing nothing on my name but only hope and the little pride I had left. I started rebuilding myself slowly, and now seven years later, I run a successful blog that helps other people in toxic relationships."

5. **You're always uneasy and restless.**

Sometimes the victim of narcissistic abuse may not know what to expect. It's hard to predict whether they'll be critical or generous. Tension might build up from constantly bracing for potential conflict if you have no idea what the other person will do or say in any given instant. Constant anxiety can result from worrying about how to respond to the onslaught of criticism and the abusive patterns you're coming to identify. You might have forgotten how to unwind because you don't feel secure enough to let your guard down.

6. You can't even recognize yourself.

Many abuse victims end up changing who they are to please their abusers. For example, let's pretend your significant other always reminds you that "when you go out with your friends, you're telling me you don't love me." Because you love them, you naturally quit spending time with your friends. Then you stop going to the gym, stop going to happy hour with your co-workers, and eventually stop seeing your sister every week. You show your lover how much you care by accommodating their interests and spending time with them. Losing your identity as a result of these transformations is a common result. You may have trouble finding happiness and will lose sight of why you're living.

Ronia Fraser, a narcissistic abusive survivor, shares how she wasn't able to recognize herself when dealing with her narcissistic husband. She documents the manipulative aspect of their relationship that made their relationship to end.

7. You struggle with establishing boundaries.

A narcissistic partner may not recognize or care about your need for space. You may face resistance while attempting to establish or maintain boundaries, and they may choose to either openly reject them or resort to silence until you give in to their demands. There comes the point when you may decide to no longer enforce any limits. You swear that you won't talk to or see your narcissistic parent again until you've broken up with them or put some distance between you. However, they may not give up readily if they believe they can wear you down over time. They'll keep phoning and texting you until you give in to them again, despite your limits. If you've ever been the victim of narcissistic abuse, you could also struggle to establish appropriate boundaries with other people.

8. **You have low self-esteem**

Living in a toxic relationship with a narcissist can often have serious consequences, including low self-esteem and depression. This is because people who are constantly put down and demeaned will often struggle to see their own worth and value. As a result, they may end up engaging in negative self-talk, comparing themselves to others, and feeling insecure about their appearance and abilities. Additionally, many narcissists use control tactics and emotional manipulation to further diminish their partner's self-worth, leaving them feeling trapped and hopeless.

Real life story:

Sarah* had been in a relationship with her narcissistic ex, Dave*, for several years before she realized how deeply he had impacted her self-esteem. Dave would constantly make derogatory comments about her looks and accomplishments, often telling her that she was incompetent or unintelligent. Over time, this verbal onslaught led Sarah to believe that none of the positive aspects of herself were real or meaningful; she saw herself as inherently flawed instead of as an individual with unique capabilities. She was in depression.

Ultimately, it took years of therapy and healing for Sarah to recognize how these toxic dynamics had affected her mentality and begin working on building up her sense of self again. Despite this process taking time, she ultimately found renewed strength from within that has helped propel her forward towards a happier life.

How Can You Get Help for Depression Caused by A Narcist in Your Life?

In dealing with Depression and anxiety, options include medication, talk therapy, and behavioral modification. Depending on the extent of the depression you are experiencing, your suggested course of treatment will vary. If your depression is moderate, your doctor may advise watching for signs of improvement before intervening. We call this "watchful waiting." In addition, they may advocate for changes in lifestyle, such as going on walks or joining support groups.

Cognitive behavioral therapy (CBT) and other talking therapies are commonly used for moderate to severe depression that is not improving. Prescriptions for antidepressants are sometimes given as well. Both conversation therapy and medications are commonly used to treat mild to severe depression. If your depression is particularly severe, you may be referred to a mental health team for more in-depth psychotherapy and medication management.

Where to look for the best therapy

Follow your doctor's orders and complete your whole course of treatment. The first few weeks of treatment can be difficult, and you may lose motivation and no longer want to continue. It may take a few months after beginning treatment for any condition to show improvement. The perception of improvement can also lead patients to discontinue treatment. Your therapist is there to help you, so feel free to open yourself to them. If not, you might want to try another. The therapist should also be informed of how you feel about the therapy sessions and the treatment plan. This allows them to engage with you and make changes if your treatment plan isn't working. It takes a few tries to find the best treatment. You should feel improvement from depression within three months of starting medication.

Talk to your doctor immediately if you have:
- No improvement in depression despite months of therapy
- Symptoms that have subsided, but you still don't feel normal
- Symptoms that are getting worse

Types of Therapies

1. **Depression Therapy**

Therapy with a reliable, trained professional may help alleviate mild to moderate depression symptoms. Therapy is often tried first by professionals before resorting to medication. However, if depression is more severe, many will try a mix of counseling and medication.

2. **Talk therapy**

In talk therapy, you and your therapist discuss your issues and feelings. Your therapist will help you identify ways of thinking or acting that add to your depression. Journaling or mood tracking could be assigned as homework. As a result, you'll be able to maintain your treatment between scheduled sessions. Your therapist may also recommend certain physical or mental activities to help you cope with your health issues and also help you prioritize them to work.

A therapist can also help you in developing plans to assist you in recognizing and avoiding situations that may bring on a relapse of depressive symptoms. As part of this process, you should work on building strategies for dealing with these triggers.

Counseling may help treat short-term or mild depression. Combined with other methods, such as medicine, it can effectively treat clinical depression.

3. Cognitive Therapy

During cognitive therapy, you work to identify and change the distorted and depressing thoughts and feelings that keep you down. This form of therapy aids patients in recognizing these unproductive thought patterns and replacing them with more positive ones. Cognitive treatment often lasts a shorter duration, from 6 weeks to 4 months.

4. Behavioral Therapy

Behavioral therapy aims to help individuals make positive changes by focusing on damaging or unhealthy behavior patterns. It operates on the premise that undesirable habits can be altered through retraining the brain. The present difficulties and their potential resolution are frequently the focal points of therapy. It is common for therapists to encourage their patients to participate in activities that will boost their spirits as part of this treatment.

5. Cognitive Behavioral therapy

Cognitive behavioral therapy, or CBT, is a popular therapeutic approach that has been shown to be particularly effective for treating depression. This type of therapy targets the underlying thoughts and behaviors that contribute to depressive symptoms, helping individuals to learn new coping strategies and break the cycle of negative thinking patterns. For example, one common CBT technique involves actively challenging negative thoughts about oneself, such as feelings of worthlessness or incompetence. In this way, CBT can help individuals to transform their relationship with depression by providing them with the tools they need to heal and move forward.

6. Antidepressant Medications

Antidepressants are the primary pharmaceutical option for treating Depression. When someone is going through a moderate to severe depressive episode, their doctor may recommend antidepressant medication and talking therapy. When alternative therapies have failed, or psychological treatments are not an option because of the severity of the problem or a lack of access to the treatment, antidepressants may be administered.

Medication is usually required for severe depression (bipolar illness and psychosis). Mood stabilizers, antipsychotics, and antidepressants are all possible options. Numerous antidepressant options are available. Choosing the right antidepressant for an individual might be difficult. A medical professional is consulted for an informed opinion before a final determination is reached. At least two weeks of taking antidepressants before you feel any improvement is typical, and it may take some trial and error with your doctor to discover the right combination of drugs and dose. The use of antidepressants can help people feel better, but they will not alter a person's character or make them permanently happy.

7. Lifestyle Changes for Depression

Depression and the stress that might amplify it can be alleviated by adopting healthier lifestyle habits like:

- Being creative by making art, journaling, and practicing yoga or mindfulness.
- Therapies such as massage, acupuncture, and light therapy are also worth a try.

- Making some adjustments to your routine may help alleviate your depression symptoms. These are most effective when used in tandem with therapy.
- To maintain optimal physical and mental health, getting adequate sleep is crucial.
- Reducing or eliminating alcohol and drug usage can significantly affect Depression.

While alcohol and drugs may provide momentary relief from depressive symptoms, they might make things worse once their effects wear off. And they can make your depression even harder to treat.

- Eating well and maintaining an active lifestyle can improve your mood and well-being.

Alterations to your diet can improve your disposition by lowering inflammation and supplying your brain with the nutrition it needs to operate optimally.

- **Exercise regularly.**

Since exercise improves the mood (from feel good hormones) and energizes you, those with depression can greatly benefit physiologically from exercising. Exercising can help you feel fantastic by reducing stress.

Practice these lifestyle tips for a less depressed life.

8. **Join Support Groups**

Individuals who have had similar occurrences or circumstances can find comfort and understanding in a support group. Cancer, long-term illness, addiction, loss, and caring are all examples of experiences that many people share. The support group members can open up to one another and talk about their feelings and coping strategies and any knowledge they may have about the disease or therapy being received.

Many patients find that the lack of emotional support during medical treatment can be mitigated by joining a health-related support group. The emotional support a patient receives from their doctor and other medical staff, as well as from their friends and family, may not be sufficient. The gap between physical and psychological care may be bridged by joining a support group with others who have had a similar experience. Non-profits, medical facilities, and community centers are some possible support group hosts. They could also operate autonomously, with no oversight from outside parties. Meetings for support groups can take many forms, from in-person get-togethers to teleconferences and online forums. Support group members generally share a common set of emotions, fears, issues, daily challenges, treatment decisions, or treatment-related side effects due to their shared experiences. Being in a group allows you to interact with others who are more likely to have similar goals and they become your support when things are not well.

How Can People with Depression Related to NPD (Narcist) Improve Their Quality of Life?

1) Staying Active by Rediscovering Themselves

When depressed, it's common to lose interest in once-favorite pastimes. It's also possible to assume that you won't enjoy something, only to find that you have more fun than anticipated after you start. Not participating in potential depression relievers limits your options. You can boost the number of things you look forward to doing by:

• Write down all the things you used to like to do and write this in great detail, going back to your childhood so as to rediscover past passions.

• Schedule at least one of these events every day.

• Create time for things you value most.

• After participating in an event, reflect on and/or record your favorite parts.

• Inquire of others about what kinds of things they enjoy doing.

2) Maintain a regular sleep routine

Sleep problems are a common symptom of depression. You should sleep the way you used to for recovery purposes. You can do the following to improve your sleep:

- Consistently follow a regular bedtime and wake time.
- If worries make you toss and turn at night, schedule some time during the day to work through them.
- Do not consume caffeinated beverages (including coffee, strong tea, cola, or energy drinks) after 4 p.m., and limit yourself to two cups of these beverages daily.
- Don't use alcohol as a sleep ai because it reduces sleep quality and increases waking hours are side effects of alcohol metabolism.
- Relax before bedtime and give yourself time to unwind. Stop working or studying at least half an hour before night and do something soothing.
- Put your phone in another room at night and give your mind a vacation from online activities like social media for at least an hour before bedtime.

3) Think of positive things

Depressed persons often worry or dwell on bad thoughts. As a result, you will have a harder time recovering from your injuries and be more susceptible to negative feelings.

Here are some suggestions that may help you relax and think more positively:

- Jot down your concerns and write them down. Think critically about how plausible your worries are. Find out what other people have thought about this and why.
- Avoid dwelling on what is out of your control.
- Remember to be in the here and now. Learn to accept your thoughts without giving them any attention.
- Make a list of your issues and possible solutions. You should write down the benefits and drawbacks of each choice and pick the one that seems most viable. Analyze the situation to see if the solution worked.

4) Learn to Control Anger

Irritability is a common symptom of depression. Alterations to one's sleeping and eating habits can aggravate these symptoms. Assist yourself in coping by doing the following:

- Let people know what's going on, especially if you've been acting unpleasant around them, to help them understand your emotions.
- To calm down if you feel your temper rising and walk away from the situation.
- Learn to relax by starting to meditate regularly. This will lessen the emotional impact of stressful events.
- Speak to trusted friends and family about your situation.
- Anxiety disorders are common among those who suffer from depression and can cause anger issues. It is crucial to seek professional help and inform your therapist if you are experiencing any anxiety symptoms so that they can appropriately help

you with treatment.

5) Write Down Your Thoughts through Journaling

Journaling is a powerful tool that can help individuals struggling with depression. By providing a space for reflection and self-expression, journaling can help to alleviate some of the symptoms of depression, such as feelings of hopelessness and despair.

This is likely due to the fact that writing encourages us to focus on our strengths and achievements, instead of fixating on our failures or shortcomings. Ultimately, journaling can be an invaluable tool for anyone who wants to overcome depression and reclaim happier, more fulfilling lives.

6) Strengthen Your Perception of Yourself

Treating depression requires focusing on the whole person, including boosting self-esteem. You can improve your outlook on life by reminding yourself of your strengths. Eating well, exercising frequently, and surrounding yourself with positive people are great ways to boost your confidence and sense of self-worth.

7) Maintain a Regular Routine

Those suffering from Depression might benefit much from establishing and sticking to a regular, healthful routine. Many times, with depression, people's motivation declines, which contributes to feelings of ineffectiveness and low self-esteem. To achieve as much equilibrium as possible in your life, schedule an activity you must perform every day and make it something you enjoy doing.

8) **Get Involved**

If you're depressed, you can feel like staying alone and resenting things you formerly enjoyed. Having a social life is crucial. Force yourself to meet with people at work, family or friends that are supportive. Maintaining positive relationships with others is an effective way to combat depression and avoid the negative effects of isolating yourself. For instance, watch a movie, take a walk, or just chat with a close friend. This will help improve your mood.

9) **Feel Good About Yourself Through Exercise**

At its core, depression is intimately linked to feelings of low self-worth and lack of motivation. These negative feelings often serve to further decrease a person's desire or ability to engage in activities they normally enjoy. However, by incorporating exercise into your routine, you can begin to break this negative cycle and start to heal from your depression. For example, studies have shown that regular physical activity helps to release feel-good hormones like serotonin and endorphins, which can then lift your mood naturally. Additionally, moving around and being more active can also help increase your energy levels and reinvigorate your brain, giving you the focus and drive needed to tackle any mental roadblocks in your way. Overall, exercising can be an incredibly effective tool for dealing with depression and restoring a sense of balance and well-being in your life. So, if you're struggling with this mood disorder, don't hesitate to start moving today!

Final Takeaway

Depression is a very real and serious illness that can be the result of being in a relationship with a narcissist. It's important to know the signs of depression so you can get help if you are feeling down or hopeless. There are many ways to overcome depression, some of which include seeking professional help and therapy, journaling, and exercising. You can also build your self-esteem by focusing on your positive qualities and taking time for yourself. If you are struggling with depression as a result of being in a narcissistic relationship, please reach out for help. You are not alone.

Chapter 5: Coping with a NPD in your life

It is quite frustrating to have a relationship with someone with a narcissistic personality. Letting go of a bad relationship, especially with a person with narcissistic behaviors, can also be challenging. Unfortunately, not everyone can leave a toxic relationship because these people are family members, spouses and even bosses at work.
How, then, do you cope and deal with a Narcissistic personality?

Take These Steps to Handle a Narcissist:

1. Clearly know why you are staying

When deciding whether to stay in a relationship with a narcissist, first and foremost, you must evaluate why you want to continue this relationship. Some common reasons people stay with a narcissist include fear of being alone or being controlled by the narcissist, desire for drama and excitement, or simply not wanting to deal with the uncertainty of breaking up. Additionally, it is crucial to assess your partner's willingness and ability to accept support from others. If your partner seems open to working on their issues and seeking out professional help, it may be possible for your relationship to move forward positively.

However, if your partner resists any efforts at intervention or refuses to seek help on their own, it may be best to end the call an end to the relationship and move on. Ultimately, only you can decide what the best action is for you and your relationship - but by staying mindful of these key considerations, so that you make an informed decision about the path forward.

2. **Stay away from confrontations**

People with NPD are extremely sensitive, especially to criticism. Therefore, telling a true narcissist, they are narcissists will worsen the situation and may backfire. You, therefore, need to become a strong-minded person and realize that your criticism may be constructive, but those with NPD will not own up to their behavior and see the truth behind the accusation.

Avoid getting into a confrontation with your grievances against them using the compliment sandwich approach. It involves you opening the conversation and closing it with positive remarks about the one you're talking to. For example, you can begin the conversation by telling them what you love about them and then say how you would love them to change a specific behavior, so they can be better people and improve your relationship. Finish the conversation by telling them how confident you are that they will be successful in changing certain behavior. This approach will lessen the brunt of feedback that will come from them.

3. **Create boundaries to protect yourself**

Boundaries are essential for maintaining your mental health and well-being in a narcissistic relationship. One good way to create boundaries is to set specific limits on how often you interact with the person. For example, if the narcissist in your life tends to constantly bombard you with texts or messages, try limiting contact to a few times a day or only when absolutely necessary. By setting clear limits and sticking to them, you can help maintain your own health while also addressing any negative behaviors exhibited by the narcissist.

4. Find time for yourself each day

Whether that means taking a walk around the block, reading a book, or going out with friends. This way, no matter the challenges in your relationship, you will always have some way to relieve the stress and take refuge in.

5. Educate yourself about NPD

When it comes to dealing with narcissistic tendencies in a partner, you need to do is become educated about this condition. After all, narcissism is a complex mental disorder characterized by an excessive sense of self and a sincere lack of empathy for others. To better understand and sympathize with your partner, learning more about the symptoms, causes, risk factors, and treatment options associated with narcissism can be helpful. For example, did you know that narcissists often struggle with feelings of doubt and sadness or sometimes experience intense feelings of shame? By gaining a deeper understanding of this condition through research, you'll be better prepared to support your loved one as he or she seeks help for their narcissistic tendencies. It will also help you understand them better and learn that this condition is not caused by you but is an internal mental issue.

6. Improve Your Communication

To effectively address problems in a relationship with a person that has narcissistic tendencies, it is important to engage in meaningful dialogues that allow for honest communication. If your partner becomes emotional or refuses to talk at certain times, try to remain calm and explain that you will address the issue once they have regained their composure. Whether you or your partner are experiencing rage, contempt, frustration, despair, or any other intense emotions, it is important to acknowledge these feelings and find constructive ways to channel them. One effective approach is encouraging your partner to communicate their feelings constructively, without anger or other destructive behaviors. Additionally, be on the lookout for attempts at manipulation by your partner, as many narcissists will use this approach as their way to trying to control the situation. By staying focused on positive communication strategies and being willing to work through difficult situations together, you can successfully navigate the complexities of a relationship with a narcissist.

7. Know that you have choices in your interaction with the person

Another key element in dealing with a narcissist is focusing on your interaction choices. For example, if you cannot break your relationship with an NPD family member, you can take measures to protect yourself so that their behaviors are less harmful to you.

You can limit your time with them and make sure someone else is always around, so you are never alone with them. Let them know that you can certainly break contact with them if certain behaviors persist and specifically state how you will respond to such behaviors.

For example, make it clear that you are willing to spend time with them, but if they come up with insulting comments about your career or spouse, you will have to leave the room. Such a technique is one of the best for dealing with a narcissist because the ball is in their court, and they have to choose whether or not to comply.

8. Know Which battles to Pick wisely

When dealing with a partner who has narcissistic tendencies, it is important to pick your battles wisely. These individuals can often be insensitive and display a tendency towards manipulative behaviors and insults. It's, therefore, very easy to get emotionally caught up in every conflict that arises. However, you must stay calm and mindful when dealing with these types of situations, tuning into your internal cues about what does or does not require a response from you.

One very effective way to do this is by setting clear boundaries for yourself. This boundary should define the kind of behavior and action that are acceptable or unacceptable in your relationship. These boundaries can help you keep your mental well-being and composure during challenging interactions with a narcissist, allowing you to focus on maintaining a healthy relationship overall.

9. **Emphasize immediate action and not promises**

People with narcissistic personalities know the art of making promises. They can promise to do what you have asked but will not do it. Most of the time, they make sincere promises, but in other cases, the promises may be a means to their end.

Although it is not recommended to confront them directly, be clear on what you expect and what you want as you express yourself calmly and gently. Make them know that you will fulfill your promises when they fulfill their promises.

10. **Create a support system**.

You are likely to have feelings of insecurity, self-doubt and confusion when living with a narcissist. Therefore, have a group of people like therapists, family and friends who can support you in maintaining your emotional wellness. Even if the therapy cannot cure your partner's narcissism, it will show you problem-solving strategies essential in dealing with a narcissist and emphasize self-care and self-love.

11. Watch out for Gaslighting

When dealing with a narcissist, you are likely to experience behaviors known as gaslighting. Gaslighting is where the person engages in manipulative behaviors and still denies reality in a way that causes him to doubt yourself.

For example:

- They will deny saying something or suggest that they were joking, but you are being sensitive.
- They will undermine your confidence when they suggest that you don't know the actual events, or they will accuse you of misinterpreting facts and overreacting to situations.
- Sometimes, they will deny the things they did or said

It's not easy to deal with gaslighting because it is your word against theirs. The perfect way to deal with this is to keep records of the event by noting them down and keeping records that corroborate your experiences.

12. Love yourself for an improved relationship

Learning to love yourself unreservedly is an important part of cultivating healthy relationships. Because our behavior toward others often reflects how we treat ourselves, those with narcissistic tendencies may have little desire to change their behavior. However, by learning to love and cherish yourself just as you would a valued friend or partner, you can begin to shift this dynamic. This does not necessarily mean that your partner will begin healing immediately, but it does provide you with the ability to take back the power to control your happiness and set an example for how you want to be treated. Whether dealing with narcissism in a romantic relationship or any other situation, having the courage and self-love to find peace is vital to creating positive change.

13. Actively boost your own self-esteem

In order to deal with people who exhibit narcissistic traits, it is important to first focus on boosting your own self-esteem. This can be done in different types of ways. One way is by engaging in positive activities that make you feel good about yourself, like taking up a new hobby or sport that allows you to connect with others and build your confidence. Surrounding yourself with loving and supportive family and friends also helps you to feel better.

For example, you might consider joining a group or community where you can tap into shared experiences and support from others facing similar challenges. Ultimately, building up your own sense of self-worth and resilience will help you better navigate difficult interactions with those who may have more narcissistic tendencies. And most importantly, remember to affirm to yourself regularly that you are worthy of love and respect just as you are.

14. Be Careful about how you interact with a Narcissist.

When coping and dealing with a narcissist, it is important to be very mindful of how you interact with them. To minimize the risk of conflict or confrontation, try to keep your interactions short and focused on the facts. By being assertive and staying calm, you can work more effectively with a narcissist without letting yourself get stressed out or upset by their behavior. Ultimately, understanding and responding appropriately to a narcissist can help you form stronger relationships both at home and in the workplace.

15. Get Professional Help

When dealing with a toxic family member who displays narcissistic behaviors, knowing where to turn for support and guidance can be difficult. That's why seeking professional help from a mental health professional may be the best option. Counseling can help to address feelings of low self-esteem, loneliness, and public humiliation while teaching you how to effectively deal with the challenging behaviors of your narcissistic family member. Whether you're looking for strategies to manage your interactions with this person or simply want a safe space to process your experiences, working with a mental health professional can be an invaluable tool to use to cope and heal. So if things ever become too difficult to handle on your own, don't hesitate to reach out for the support you need.

16. Stay away from those who don't support your decisions.

When you are in a narcissistic relationship, it is difficult to stay strong and independent. You may face pressure from friends and family who do not support your decision to stay in the relationship. These people may quietly or openly encourage you to leave or try to convince you that staying is unhealthy or unreasonable.

At times like this, it is critical to remain focused on what you know to be true: that you deserve to be in a healthy, supportive relationship. Don't let well-meaning friends or family members undermine your confidence or make you question your choices. Instead, surround yourself with people who will respect and encourage your decisions, and remember that your happiness is more important than what others think. After all, staying in a narcissistic relationship takes strength and resilience, and you should be proud of the choice that you have made.

17. Speak up for yourself

It is sometimes advisable to ignore something or walk away from it. However, the same does not apply to close relationships. For example, dealing with your spouse requires different strategies than dealing with your sibling and coworkers.

When you realize that your boundaries have been crossed by someone close to NPD, don't get visibly frustrated or show annoyance. If this is someone that you need to keep in your life, then you should speak up. However, do this calmly and gently. It would be best if you informed them of how their words impact your life and are specific about what you expect and how you want to be treated, and as you do this keep in mind that they may not understand or empathize with you.

18. Find the good in that person.

When someone has a personality disorder, it doesn't necessarily mean they are bad. They are not bad because the disorder only changes their ability to perceive reality accurately. Most of the time, it might be harder to find the good in narcissists, but with enough learning and understanding, it becomes much easier to see the good in them. Whenever you experience any thought of negativity towards them, counter it with a positive thought. Even simple statements of positivity will work well in maintaining a healthy relationship with the narcissist.

19. Understand that narcissists are not capable of changing themselves.

When in a relationship with a person who has narcissistic tendencies, it is important to understand that they are unlikely to change. According to psychology and recent scientific research, narcissism is a mental disorder that is portrayed by a lack of empathy and an inflated sense of self. Because of this, people with narcissistic tendencies often exhibit behaviors that can be harmful or abusive to those around them. Therefore, it is generally unwise to hope for a change in these behaviors or attempt to get the person to become more sympathetic or loving towards others. Instead, the best way to deal with a narcissist is simply to accept them for who they are and learn how to set healthy boundaries in your interactions with them.

By acknowledging their limitations and focusing on taking care of yourself, you can cope more effectively with the challenges that come from dealing with someone who suffers from the condition of narcissism.

Ways to handle narcissistic children.

1. Learn more about NPD.

The more you understand your children's behaviors, the easier it will be to accept them for who they are and to set your limits.

2. Set clear boundaries.

Boundaries are the reasonable space between both people's needs—your boundaries are there to protect your own needs and energy, not to change their behavior.

3. Gently draw their attention to their actions.

Narcissists frequently are unaware of how their actions affect others. When it is safe to do so, gently pointing these out helps them learn what is and is not acceptable behavior when they are around you.

4. Accept that which you cannot change.

A narcissistic personality disorder is a complex and often chronic illness that can be changed or mitigated. Please recognize that you cannot make your children change but can influence the degree of narcissism carefully.

When To Leave a Relationship with A Narcissist Spouse.

Toxic relationships can be extremely detrimental to your emotional wellness and mental well-being. If staying around a narcissist is causing you distress and difficulty functioning normally, you should end the relationship. This means you need to leave the situation altogether. When the situation turns abusive and dangerous, find help as soon as possible. It will not be easy for a narcissist to change on their own and if the cycle of abuse continues, letting go of a bad relationship is the best solution.

Final Takeaway

So, these are some ways that you can deal with a narcissist. It's important to remember that it's not your responsibility to change or fix the narcissist – only they can do that. You can, however, take steps to protect yourself and get some relief from their behavior. By creating boundaries, finding time for yourself, watching out for gaslighting, not arguing with them and other tips mentioned above, you can make it through this difficult time. If you find that you're struggling to cope, don't hesitate to reach out for help from a professional. And lastly, be sure to build a strong support system of friends and family who will understand what you're going through and offer practical and emotional support. If you're in contact with a narcissist outside the home, our next chapter will share how to cope!

Chapter 6: How to Deal with a Narcissist Outside the Home

Having to interact with a narcissist may be quite draining and frustrating. It can be stressful and disruptive to your daily life, making it hard to relax at home or work. It's crucial to find ways to deal with it. You may better manage your connection with the narcissist while protecting your mental health if you take the time to investigate what motivates narcissists and try out some crucial coping tactics.

Ways to Deal with a Narcissistic Co-worker

These guidelines are useful whether you're dealing with a narcissist in your work, or social life.

1. Recognize gaslighting and understand what it can do

Gaslighting is psychological abuse in which someone questions their sense of reality. Manipulation, coercion, deliberate lying, and scapegoating are common. Knowing what gaslighting is will help you avoid being caught off guard by a coworker's behavior.

You may have experienced gaslighting at the hands of a narcissist. Individuals who manipulate in this way deny the reality that makes you question your sanity and the integrity of your own experiences.

Here's an illustration:

They could say you're being oversensitive or didn't say what you think they did. Your self-assurance could be damaged if they say things like, *"You don't know what happened,"* or *"You're misinterpreting or overreacting to the issue."* They may flat-out reject any wrongdoing or evade responsibility in other situations.

Fighting gaslighting is difficult, especially when it comes down to your word against theirs.

As a coping mechanism, you can document what happens by maintaining a journal, archiving printed documents that back up your claims, or having third parties witness any discussions you have with the other person. This is especially crucial in the job, where a narcissist trying to boost their status by smearing yours could falsely accuse you of poor performance. Make it obvious that you know their attempts to gaslight you and will not allow it to continue- part of setting boundaries.

2. Try not to take everything personally.

When it comes to dealing with difficult colleagues, it can be easy to take things personally. After all, their behavior can often affect your mood and productivity at work. But it's important to remember that this isn't necessarily a reflection on you, and that their unsavory personality may be the result of their own insecurities rather than something inherently "wrong" with you. At the end of the day, when you're dealing with a narcissist, remind yourself that you are not at fault and don't take what they say or do personally. With this approach, you'll hopefully be able to rise above any negativity and focus on thriving professionally rather than simply surviving. Because at the end of the day, success is everything – even if there are people out there that may try to stand in your way!

3. Establish firm boundaries.

When establishing boundaries with a narcissistic co-worker, it is essential to remain firm and clear in your communication. This can sometimes be challenging, especially if you have come to rely on this person for critical support or advice in the past. However, it is vital that you stay mindful of your own needs and well-being, and take steps to establish and maintain clear boundaries with this person.

One approach that can help to ensure success is to clearly define the behaviors and interactions that are acceptable and unacceptable in your professional relationship. This may involve setting specific timeframes or limits around collaboration or communication, as well as communicating which topics are off-limits or require permission before being broached. Additionally, it is important to be assertive and not hesitate to speak up whenever you feel that your boundaries are being violated or disregarded.

Ultimately, it may take some time and practice to effectively communicate your expectations and enforce healthy boundaries with a narcissistic co-worker. But by staying focused on your own needs and speaking up for yourself consistently, you can ensure that your professional relationships bring value rather than toxicity into your life.

4. Do not engage in gossip.

While there are many benefits to maintaining good relationships with your coworkers, it is equally important to refrain from engaging in gossip. Gossiping can be extremely harmful, not just to the individuals being discussed, but also to your overall ability to communicate and collaborate effectively. For instance, someone with a narcissistic streak may easily misinterpret any comments you make about other people or situations as an attack on them personally. If this occurs, they may try to use what you said against you or even turn it around and use it against others. In addition, gossip can also create tension in the workplace and poison the atmosphere for everyone involved.

To avoid these issues, it is crucial that you focus on practicing good communication skills at all times. This starts by choosing your words carefully and avoiding direct confrontation at all costs. Overall, by taking care to keep the lines of communication open and positive, you reduce the chances of falling prey to gossip.

5. Try and learn about NPD

If you know your co-worker has a narcissistic personality, you may have noticed that they are often described as attractive and likable, making it easy to overlook their other potentially dangerous tendencies. It is essential to learn to recognize the symptoms of NPD, though. As the person's strengths and flaws become clearer, and you'll be more equipped to handle any difficulties. This might be the first step toward accepting them for who they are and having more reasonable expectations for your relationship. Consult an expert in the mental health field or read blogs and books authored by experts for better understanding of this personality.

6. Be assertive and make your voice heard.

Select your battles, right? Doing nothing sometimes can be a good option. Different approaches may be needed in your approach to a parent, or spouse as opposed to a coworker or boss. If you are speaking with someone with NPD and feel that your boundaries have been broken, try not to react, get overtly upset, or exhibit annoyance. If it's someone you value and want to maintain in your life, you owe it to yourself to say something. Do your best to maintain a serene, peaceful demeanor. You must let them know how their words and actions affect you. Try to be clear and consistent about what you won't tolerate, but know that it may be difficult for them to comprehend your perspective.

7. Set Clear Boundaries

Boundaries are often disregarded while interacting with someone who has NPD. Setting clear limits about what kind of behavior is unacceptable to you is preferable to try to change someone with NPD. If you want to be taken seriously, you must set limits and stick to them instead of making empty threats.

For example:

Let's say a Jerry, a coworker frequently parks his big truck in a spot that prevents you from easily reversing out of it. To begin, politely but firmly request Jerry to give you some space. Then, make it clear what will happen if your requests are disregarded. Such instance, you'll have his car towed if you can't safely back out. It is important to do something about it the next time this happens, like calling a towing service and letting him know that they are on the way.

8. Avoid Direct Confrontations

Calling a true Narcissist a narcissist usually backfires and escalates the issue since persons with NPD are particularly sensitive to criticism. People with NPD cannot correctly adequate self-reflection to recognize the validity of an accusation, regardless of how well-meaning or helpful the critic may be. Rather, they'll be fixated on disproving your innocence and demanding an apology. To the extent that you feel compelled to bring it up, you should do it in the most effective way possible.

Someone with NPD will only respond to criticism if it is presented in little doses and heavily sugarcoated. Start the conversation on a positive note by complimenting them before venting your frustrations. Particularly, "the compliment sandwich," in which you commend the other person at the beginning and end of a conversation, can be effective. For instance, you may start by telling them what you appreciate about them and then suggest some ways they could strengthen your relationship by altering their behavior. At last, express your faith in their ability to implement these reforms.

Ways To Deal with A Narcissistic Boss.

If you're stuck with a narcissistic boss, don't worry - you're not alone. Here are some tips to help you deal with them.

1. Remind yourself of your worth regularly.

Remember your skill set, qualifications, and references that led you to seek out and secure this valuable position. Your true worth is entirely in your hands and no one else's.

2. Give them frequent compliments.

It is possible to coexist with a narcissistic boss. They enjoy receiving compliments and may expect or demand such attention and recognition. You're likelier to stay on the narcissist's good side if you're willing to provide such flattery."

3. Build your network.

Make contacts with other company leaders. However, do not reveal these actions to your narcissistic boss, who may feel slighted and enraged. It is a delicate but critical mission for your aspirations to grow in your workplace or career.

4. Broaden your work experience.

You can have a variety of supervisors who can be references for future jobs if you have opportunities to work with other leaders. Getting exposure from others also provides you with leverage when it comes to building social capital at work.

5. Consult with a labor law expert.

Speaking with a third-party expert outside your company can give you some leverage and advice on proceeding when you feel your rights are violated by your boss.

6. Work on Your Self-esteem

One of the ways a narcissist boosts their self-esteem is by putting down those around them. This can be especially hurtful if they constantly put you down not so subtly. If you work on your self-esteem, you'll be more equipped to deal with the challenging behaviors that may arise in your relationship with a boss who has NPD.

You can build your self-esteem through activities like positive self-talk, self-care, and surrounding yourself with supportive people. Maintaining a strong sense of self-worth in the face of adversity is crucial for maintaining the emotional and psychological reserves necessary for coping. When dealing with a narcissist's more destructive interpersonal behaviors, it can be helpful to maintain a healthy sense of self-worth and an authoritative position, even if the narcissist is actively trying to manipulate and undermine you.

7. Recognize When You Need Help

Dealing with a chronically self-absorbed person can tax your emotional and physical well-being. See a primary care physician first if you experience symptoms of anxiety, depression, or unexplained medical illnesses caused by a difficult boss in your life. After receiving medical care, you may inquire about being referred to other resources, such as mental health professionals and support groups. Get in touch with your loved ones and ask them for help. Don't try to tackle this problem on your own.

Final Takeaway

So, you've found yourself working with or for a narcissist. Maybe it's your colleague who always has to be the center of attention, or your boss who is constantly putting others down. No matter what role they play in your life, dealing with a narcissist can be difficult and frustrating. use the tips in this chapter to create boundaries with a narcissist, watch out for gaslighting behavior, get professional help if needed, and build up a support system. With consistency, you will manage the situation and maintain your sanity!

In our next chapter we shall discuss the process of leaving a toxic relationship. Stay tuned!

Chapter 7: How to Leave a Toxic Relationship

Breaking up with a narcissist is probably one of the most difficult things you'll ever have to do. Narcissists need their supply of the individuals they may exploit for their benefit. When they can't get what they want or need from the world, they mistreat and manipulate others to prove to themselves that they're superior. Leaving a toxic relationship with a narcissist is difficult because you will be fatigued from the love bombing, gaslighting, and frequent arguments. However, it's doable if you listen to your instincts, set clear limits, and constantly remind yourself why you need to separate. You need to know the process outlined in this chapter to secure your safety and leave the abusive narcissist behind for good.

Why It's So Difficult to End Narcissist Relationship?

Sometimes it can be very difficult to let go of bad relationship especially if they are close to you. Narcissists have the potential to be engaging, entertaining, and energizing companions. Narcissist start their relationship with you by love bombing, where they focus entirely on you, showering you with compliments and even gifts. It's natural to feel a strong desire to spend the rest of your life with them and to seek constant reassurance and approval from them during this time. However, their likable qualities gradually wane or vanish, replacing them with or interweaving hostility, criticism, demands, and narcissistic abuse to varying degrees.

Suddenly, you experience constant attacks on your sense of dignity and autonomy. Accusations and deception can lead to gaslighting, in which you start to question your sanity. You risk being assaulted, intimidated, or led astray if you speak up. You become less assertive and more submissive as time goes on. You do and allow things you would never have considered when you first met. It's like cognitive dissonance and denial have taken a hold of you. As your confidence decreases, you feel more and more ashamed. What happened to the joyful, honorable, and assured person you used to be?

Real-life Story

How things flipped from tender love to vicious manipulation

The beginning of the relationship was intoxicating. Victor* could constantly call and text Lucy*, bombarding her with admiration. Some part of her felt suspicious at this level of love intensity in a very short time. However, she decided to disregard that part because the attention was amazing. Also, Lucy had been single for a long time and imagined that this made sense and Victor could be her soulmate.

At first, the flow of validation and the adoration made it too easy for Lucy to trust him. She started sharing all her secrets with him because she felt safe with him. Victor was never judgmental but always concerned, and Lucy perceived this as genuine empathy. However, this empathy was an act of manipulation. Since narcissists don't empathize with anyone, most are masters of manipulation and can easily fake it, especially if you are desperate in love.

When Lucy was deeply hooked up, things started changing. Everything that she had told him in confidence was now being used against her. That's when she realized that narcissists use your vulnerabilities as a weapon. Victor used everything against her - from her childhood sexual abuse to her fears of abandonment and many weaknesses.

Lucy was reeling in shock at how quickly things turned this way because, one time, she was enjoying the sweetness of finding love, and the next moment, she was defending herself against Victors vicious attacks.

Lucy was desperate to get his grace back and she decided to put my brain to task and find out what she had done wrong. She felt like his approval was her heroine, she needed it desperately. The circle of abuse continued for years, and Lucy started drinking alcohol to cope. She couldn't focus on her work or her relationships. Only her family and friends' support got her to a therapist that finally helped her end the relationship. It was not easy ending the relationship because on several attempts to call it quits, Victor always had the words that made her go back to him, always making her believe that it was her fault. Lucy had an illusion that if she could stop behaving in a way that was hurting him, he would love her correctly. She later learned that the narcissist used "gaslighting" to manipulate. In the end, Lucy finally broke up with Victor and went full no contact.

A lot of damage was done when she left the relationship because she had a new issue to address - alcohol abuse. It took her about four years to trust herself enough to allow another relationship in her life. She had lost her confidence, self-worth, and ability to trust her perceptions and instincts. She now advises anyone that if they sense that they are in a narcissistic relationship, they should get out as fast as they can.

How to Leave a Toxic Relationship

1. **You shouldn't give them "just one more chance."**

When it comes to trying to leave an abusive relationship, it is important not to give the narcissist "just one more chance." Experts say that on average, it takes women seven attempts before they are able to successfully walk away from an abusive partner. This is due in part to the fact that narcissists often use behaviors such as manipulation and threats in order to try to entice you back into the relationship. They may also be extremely controlling, and their volatile or violent tendencies can make them difficult to predict. Therefore, if your partner isn't ready to end the relationship, they may resort to emotional displays such as crying and begging, in order to persuade you to stay. Ultimately, this type of behavior is just another way for the narcissist to continue exerting control over you, and giving them yet another opportunity risks further harm and even danger. So, when it comes to leaving a narcissist behind for good, remember: do not give them "just one more chance."

2. Keep your departure a secret.

While this may go against common sense, the toxic person will do one of two things after saying it. Either they will begin love bombing you in the hopes of trauma bonding and keeping you emotionally imprisoned in the relationship, or their toxic actions will escalate, posing a greater risk to your health, safety, and reputation.

3. Create an extra copy of everything you need to keep.

This is especially critical if you are a foreign national, as your abuser may try to prevent your escape by hiding your identification documents. Narcissists are notorious for taking your belongings. Find your passport if they have it. It would be helpful, at least, if you could find it, photograph it, and send those images to yourself via email. Gather all the documentation you can, such as utility bills and bank statements.

4. Don't forget to save some money.

Make sure you have your bank account established before you leave that the abuser does not know of. Plan to save an amount you will need to live on for at least 3 months after you leave.

If they are a financial abuser, you'll need to do this discreetly to prevent them from cutting off all of your funds.

5. Tell someone about what has occurred to you.

Though going to the police may be the last thing on your mind right now, speaking with a physician instead of law enforcement is good. You can say, *"I need your help; I've been abused and I was told I need to speak to my doctor."* Even if your doctor hasn't received specific training in domestic abuse, they probably know what to do. They may be able to help you find a depression or anxiety support group. If you ever need to make a case, having this documentation on hand will be very helpful.

6. Log out of all your accounts.

You should keep track of all the sites where you might have joined up, entered credit card information, or enabled auto-fills, and then delete the accounts regularly.

Another essential tip is to have a "burner" phone on hand. These phones are affordable, have no contract and ownership record and typically don't need to be charged for a year or longer. They are an ideal choice if your abuser will likely follow you or try to monitor your whereabouts after you leave.

Finally, it's important to scan any devices that you use often, such as your computer or phone, for any tracking software that may be installed. Once you identify any potential spyware, take steps to remove it right away. Whether it's changing passwords or updating your browser settings, doing so will help ensure that your abuser cannot continue to pry into your life without your knowledge.

These proactive approaches towards escaping a narcissist, can help you to create the space needed to reclaim control over yourself and your life.

7. Do not fall for their flattery.

To prevent their victims from leaving, "narcissists try to employ extreme flattery or greater abuse." The ultimate goal is to make the abused person feel like they have no option but to stay in the abusive relationship since it has become everything they've ever wanted.

To truly escape a narcissist, you must cut off all communication with them because narcissists can be very charming, making it difficult to leave. After you break up, your ex may resort to manipulating you relentlessly. If your ex does manage to get in touch with you, ignore any guilt trips, apologies, or other attempts at manipulation. You should consider filing a police report if your ex-partner begins to harass you by showing up at your place of employment or residence or following you around public places. You shouldn't waste more energy or emotions on your ex.

You deserve a partner who won't toy with your feelings.

8. Find time to talk to your loved ones again.

Abusive narcissists seek to isolate their victims from their support systems, so it's possible that you haven't seen some of your closest friends and family members in a long time. Since the narcissist probably didn't want you spending time with anyone else, they may have managed to turn you against them by spreading lies and creating an atmosphere of terror. You shouldn't be concerned about how they'll respond when they meet you again or how ashamed or afraid you might feel.

Many victims have been socialized to feel that their peers simply won't accept them. It only implies you were deceived, and anyone can be tricked; changing your frame of reference is all it takes. It's more widespread than you think, and individuals may have wanted to help you but didn't know how to help you out of a lack of knowledge or confidence.

9. Don't just leave; Stay Away.

When you finally leave, you might feel the urge to return. When we leave a toxic relationship, including one with a narcissist, our brains are adept at making us recall all the good times and blocking out all the bad. It's not enough to just leave; you must ensure you never return. You should know that the happy times you spent with them that led you to believe in their potential were almost all lies. A narcissist is skilled at pretending to be decent, which is part of the problem. The narcissist will try to keep you by playing on your emotions. They'll apologize, and they may try to surprise you on your birthday when they know you'll be vulnerable, or, if you have a shared past, they may tell you on their special day that they miss you and everything you used to do together. Keep in mind that these are all tricks.

10. You need to learn some grounding techniques.

If you've recently emerged from a traumatic situation, such as an abusive relationship, it's crucial to take some time to center yourself. Your brain's timekeeper is not working effectively, making you think the past is the present. This implies that the past's sights, sounds, and tastes can all be recreated with remarkable accuracy. It's like post-traumatic stress disorder, which you must fight through if you don't want it to consume your life. That's why it's crucial that you "reclaim yourself," Discover the root of your attraction to this person and free yourself from their spell.

11. Create a list to remind you why you left

If the narcissist continues to stalk you, fortifying yourself is essential. Keep a running tally of all the wrongs done to you on your phone, so you can quickly reference the wrongs if necessary. Whenever that message alert sounds on your phone, read that list. That will convince you, believe it or not. They may send heartfelt letters causes an influx of oxytocin and a feeling of warmth and fuzziness in your brain and emotions. However, remember that it's not genuine; if you sympathize with your abuser, you won't have any compassion left over for yourself.

Study the reasons why you left and ask yourself why you tolerate them. You wouldn't put up with someone mistreating your family, so you shouldn't put up with it yourself. Breaking up with a narcissist can be challenging. Keeping in touch with a narcissist ex invites manipulation, guilt, and gaslighting. When you depart, cut all ties immediately. You should unfriend and ban your ex on all social networking sites and block their phone number and email. If you need to maintain contact with your ex for the sake of your children, you should think carefully about how to do so.

12. Get Professional Help

Seeing a therapist after breaking up with a narcissist can be very beneficial. A significant number of persons who have been in relationships with narcissists report low self-esteem and confidence due to their experiences. Trusting others at this time may be difficult, and you may feel overwhelmed and bewildered. Even if it's for the best in the long term, ending a relationship can still bring up many feelings. Leaving a narcissist is a healthy decision and share with the therapist so as to heal and move past this dark time.

13. Connect with a Support Group on Narcissistic Survivors

Isolating the victim from their support system is a hallmark of narcissistic abuse. There's a chance you won't be able to trust people as easily as you once did. On the other hand, it's likely that they still care about you and would like to assist you in narcissistic abuse recovery if they can. Take the time to reconnect with old friends and acquaintances and make new ones that can serve as a solid foundation of support. If you don't have somebody close to you who can help you, you can benefit from connecting with others who have been through something similar by attending a support group. Having those who have been through something similar and can offer advice and comfort can be a great help during recovery from a narcissist.

14. With shared parental responsibility, pick your conflicts wisely.

When dealing with a narcissistic ex-partner, it is important to choose your conflicts wisely. Although having shared parental responsibility can be challenging at times, it is important to remember that the wellbeing of your children should be your top priority. By keeping an open mind and understanding the root causes of your ex's behavior, you can work together to ensure that your children are well cared for in all aspects of their lives. Whether you are negotiating visitation schedules or planning major decisions regarding their care, always put your children first and stay focused on what is best for them, rather than getting bogged down in conflict with your ex. With patience and dedication, you can successfully navigate the ups and downs of co-parenting with a narcissistic partner.

Final Takeaway

So, these are some steps that you can take to help make the process of leaving a Narcissist partner a little bit easier on yourself. Remember, it's important to stay strong and focused during this time, and to reach out for support from your loved ones whenever possible. If you find that you are struggling more than you feel capable of handling alone, don't be afraid to seek professional help. And finally, once you have made the decision to leave, remember to stay away from them to protect yourself emotionally and mentally.

In our next chapter we shall address the healing process from a Narcissistic relationship. There is hope!

Chapter 8: Healing After A Breakup With A Narcissist

Having an intimate relationship with someone with narcissistic traits can bring many challenges. However, narcissistic abuse comes in different stages; you may not know you are getting into a relationship with a narcissist. You may fall deeply in love with them and then find a challenge getting out of the relationship when things start going south. Here's a good explanation of the Narcissistic Abuse Cycle that happens in 4 steps.

Understanding the Narcissistic Abuse Cycle

The cycle of abuse in a narcissistic relationship is characterized by repeated and escalating cycles of idealization, devaluation, discarding and hoovering.

Idealization occurs when a narcissist is initially drawn to their partner due to how they perceived them to be, often imagining them to be perfect or more than capable. However, as time passes, the narcissist's feelings towards their partner slowly change from admiration and adoration to contempt and anger.

This is known as devaluation, where the narcissist begins to see their partner as inherently flawed or unworthy. As this devaluation intensifies, the narcissist may begin to lash out at their partner or even discard them completely. This can take one of two extreme forms: either the narcissist ends the relationship suddenly and without warning, or they instead begin deftly manipulating their significant other using tricks to keep a grasp of their victim in a process called hoovering. The end result is always the same: a broken relationship and an empty sense of betrayal on the victim's part. In order to heal from such abuse once it has occurred, victims must seek professional help to process this toxic pattern and move forward with hope for a brighter future.

Overcoming Abuse By A Narcissist After Divorce

It is challenging, and it's normal to feel sadness and uncertainty over ending the relationship. According to research, post-divorce from narcissistic abuse can be followed by changes in how your brain processes emotions. However, it would be best if you were easy on yourself because you need to stand strong for your needs. Toxic relationship recovery involves a period of healing that has no time limit.

Stages of Healing from A Narcissist After Divorce

1. The Denial Stage

When you start experiencing narcissist abuse and find out how it affects you, that's the beginning of your recovery and to start feeling happier. The denial stage takes place during the relationship. When the intensity of the initial stages of the relationship starts fading away, you start noticing that your narcissistic partner has changed. The love and affection are not like in the beginning. They may start ignoring you, lashing out in anger, or insulting you. For example, they may go to the extent of telling you that your friends are not good for you. At first, you will be in denial that your relationship is facing a problem. You tell yourself that your partner is simply having a bad day, and the living partner will emerge when that is over.

2. The Guilt Stage

At this stage, you start seeing the narcissist for who they are. You realize your partner is abusive and manipulative and feel guilty for falling for them. Additionally, you will blame yourself for not seeing the red flags- warning signs- and for trusting them enough and falling for their charm at the beginning of the relationship. At this stage, you start experiencing low self-esteem and can't even manage to take the first step toward leaving your partner.

3. The Bargaining Stage

You are stuck in a relationship with the narcissist at this stage. You are unwilling to end things because you are convincing yourself that they'll change if you try harder. You may try showering them with attention, being cautious to avoid upsetting them or putting all your time and energy into becoming the perfect partner. In your mind, you believe that you are the source of the problem, and if you fix some of the flaws, the narcissist will return to being the love of your life, like when you first met.

4. Grieving and Depression

At this point, the actions of the narcissist are very evident. You now start feeling your one-sided relationship and how exploitative it is. You now realize that the narcissist never loved you and lied to you into becoming their support system, the loving partner, without reciprocating. When you realize this, you experience deep sadness, as the relationship is not savable. It dawned on you that you have been in love with someone incapable of loving you, and you now understand that you must end it.

5. The Turning Point

In this stage, you stop fixating on the narcissist and fix the relationship. You have overcome the sadness and fear holding you in the relationship. You are now ready to take steps to leave the narcissist. You want to stop being worried and start healing your heart. This which usually involves cutting off contact with the narcissist and starting over a new. At this stage, you are focused on healing your attachment to the narcissist and embark on a journey of emotional well-being.

6. Working through the Pain Stage

At this stage, you have divorced the narcissist and cut off contact. Here, you are at liberty to heal and process your emotions which is the beginning of the post-divorce stage. Now that you are detached, it is time to stand strong to your needs through self-reflection. Reflect on the circumstances that made you form a relationship with the narcissist. Find out if there were any early red flags that you missed.

Remember that the narcissistic abuse was never your fault. Still, recognizing any warning signs you may have missed can make your stay careful not to land in a similar situation in the future.

Be easy on yourself during this stage. You are likely to find that occasional feeling of sadness emerges, and you can start missing the narcissist at some point.

Challenges may also arise with processing emotions. For example, you may start reacting poorly to upsetting situations since your brain is still alert to narcissistic abuse.

7. Create Hope for the Future

This stage is where healing your attachment wounds begin.

It begins when you stop worrying because you have had an opportunity to process your emotions and are ready to start feeling happier with a positive mindset. You might even be ready to enter another relationship after narcissistic abuse because you have completed healing yourself.

At this stage, you can accept your role in attracting a narcissist. You may have failed to set boundaries or had unhealed childhood trauma that led you to an abusive person. You now recognize your faults while understanding that narcissists are accountable for their behavior.

As you proceed through the stages of healing after narcissistic abuse, giving yourself time and space to recover is important. You have gone through significant mistreatment by a narcissist, and you may have signs of PTSD.

The process of healing from narcissistic abuse requires that you recognize that you will need to make some changes. Some of the changes may require you to learn how to set boundaries, stand strong to your needs and stop being a people pleaser.

Additionally, taking time for self-care and knowing how to stop anxiety is crucial which comes with trying a new relationship. When you begin to care for your own needs, you will realize that you're in a better position to work on your healing from narcissistic abuse.

How to Heal After a Narcissistic Relationship

There are guidelines that you can follow that the recovery process focuses on. The following tips will help you to heal and rediscover yourself and feel better after encountering a narcissist.

1. Acknowledging and accepting the abuse

Leaving a narcissistic relationship can be an incredibly difficult and painful process. During this time, it is important to acknowledge and accept the abuse that you have experienced in order to begin the healing process. This can involve reaching out to supportive friends and family members, seeking professional counseling or therapy, and journaling about your thoughts and feelings.

Another key aspect of accepting in recovery involves gaining a deeper understanding of what motivated your former partner's harmful behavior. Often times, people who exhibit narcissistic behaviors were victims of emotional or physical abuse themselves, which can help to bring greater compassion to their damaging actions. By getting to the root of their pain, we can begin to better understand how they may have used abusive tactics as a misguided attempt at self-protection.

As you work through the healing process, remember that you are not alone. There are many others who have been through similar experiences and can offer support along the way. With time, patience, and courage, it is possible to leave your narcissistic relationship behind once and for all – and begin living the life you deserve!

2. Get your identity back.

Narcissists always expect others to behave in a specific way. They can harshly belittle or criticize you for failing to meet their standards. They may try to control your time and stop you from seeing your friends or participating in activities.

Post-divorce, you may have stopped doing the things you love because of manipulation, and you may feel that you no longer know yourself very well. You can go back to what used to interest you as a young person. This will help you to start feeling more like yourself again and slowly regain your identity. Happiness is the key to toxic relationship recovery, and getting your identity back will help you heal from the narcissist after divorce.

3. Understand that your feelings may linger

Despite the sharp pain and lingering emotions that may accompany divorce, it is important to remember that you have the power to begin healing your broken heart. Even if you still love your former partner, it doesn't mean that you need to remain in an unhealthy or toxic relationship. By recognizing the behaviors that caused harm and continuing to work on your own healing, you can start to move forward from the past and focus on building a better future for yourself. With time and patience, you can learn to let go of the hurt and find peace in your heart once again.

4. Talk to your friends.

Opening up to friends and family members who can support you will help heal and regain your life. Friends and family that care about you will:

- Offer compassion and listening ear
- Provide you company in your difficult days
- Remind you that whatever happened to you wasn't your fault

Remember, some people may not offer much (or any) support and might take the abusive person's side. For example, mutual friends may support an abusive ex's actions.

When this happens, you will feel hurt. It's often important to set boundaries around your time with such people as you work on healing your life and body. For example, ask them not to talk about the person around you or not to share their opinions about the situation with you. If they do not respect those boundaries, consider limiting your time with them.

5. Defuse your fear.

It is important to immediately work on your level of fear and learn how to stop anxiety. The rage of narcissists can be awful and frightening at the same time. The narcissist plans to make you feel worried, anxious and threatened. When they do this, they ensure that you don't think straight and you will easily give in to what they want.

 A narcissist believes that you have to feel bad for making them look like a failure or making them feel like a failure. Therefore, a humiliated narcissist can be very intimidating. It would be best if you didn't believe the narcissist's predictions and ignored their threats. Always protect yourself both physically and psychologically. The steps that you take to protect yourself will help in diffusing fear. For example, begin the divorce process and remove your name from all the joint accounts.

Additionally, you should not seek help from the narcissist as much as you need it. Moreover, avoid responding to hostile emails and texts and keep copies of verbal and written threats in your notebook. These threats can be given to the police if you fear for you and your children's lives. The sooner you do these things, the sooner you start feeling stronger.

6. **Breathe intentionally.**

Breathing intentionally may sound simple, but paying attention to breathing is important. When experiencing fear, you are likely to stop breathing or hyperventilate. Such reactions will interfere with the oxygen reaching your heart, brain and other organs. If you don't breathe properly, it triggers a freeze response. When your brain and body freeze, you will not remember things, can't think properly, and can't make rational decisions.

Sometimes you will find yourself considering to go back to the narcissist or even beg them to come back so that they can ease your panic and fear. However, breathing normally is essential for you to catch your thoughts and flying emotions about calling them.

Here is how you should breathe;

- Sit or lay down somewhere comfortable and quiet.
- Put your hand on your heart and the other one on your diaphragm.
- Breathe slowly as you feel both hands moving out when your lungs fill with air for a count of 4
- Now slowly breathe out to another count of 4. Make sure to allow your lungs to deflate and your shoulders to drop.
- Repeat these 5 to 6 times to help you clear your mind.

Most people who have tried this breathing technique find it very relaxing to breathe normally. If deeply stressed, repeat this for 5 to 10minutes.

The exercise brings your cognitive functions back online. Relaxation or sleep medication may be helpful if your body stays tense that you find breathing painful or can't sleep.

When medication is used carefully, they can help you keep your panic in check. Talk with your doctor about what you are going through and ask for their best treatment and one that is right for you.

7. **Find support.**

You cannot deal with the situation you are in alone. Having someone who can listen to you will help you decompress, empty your thoughts, and regain your sanity. When you have someone to talk to, you get validation that you are sane and can handle the situation you are going through. Therefore, you can use the services of a therapist who knows about narcissists, one that is non-judgmental, a caretaker, and a best friend. These people will make a good support team.

Additionally, you can join support groups, read books on mental health, and get busy with weekly social activities. Although it may be difficult to ask for help, remember that this is a serious situation, and you need help. It is good for both emotional and physical health.

8. Disengage from the Narcissist

The number one way of protecting yourself from a hostile narcissist is by disengaging. That is what a narcissist hates, but since they are already in a rage, it is no longer your job to take care of their feelings. On the contrary, it is time to consider your emotional needs. Post-divorce, Marriage lawyers encourage their clients to stop responding or interacting with the narcissist and that they should do it through the lawyer if they have to communicate. However, some clients don't listen to them. It is important to list in your lawyer's instructions, and until a final verdict is reached, the narcissist will try to distract your mind by what they are saying, and it is important to disengage them the best way you can.

Disengaging doesn't involve only not talking to the narcissist, but it also involves emailing, texting and interacting. Additionally, it would be best to let the narcissist go emotionally by quitting thinking about what they think of you. Moreover, it would help if you let go of all the dependence on the narcissist- this involves physical and financial independence. Disengagement means you are in control of your life, and the narcissist cannot determine the feelings. After getting the narcissist out of your head, you will feel significantly better, more creative, optimistic and happier.

9. Stick to business.

When you are done disengaging with the narcissist, begin treating your interactions with them like it's a business- when you have to discuss your children. Emotional responses are put in the background when doing business, and people only discuss specific issues. You will always act cordially in a business setting, despite what you may feel for them. In a business, you may have a disagreement that does not lead to name-calling or being hostile and giving rude remarks. You never cry or beg when dealing with business associates, so why do it with the narcissist. Don't give them the pleasure of seeing you weak and frail. The interactions between you and the narcissist can significantly improve if you follow this model.

The narcissist was your most trusted and closest companion – their response mattered in whatever you did more than anybody else. However, that is gone. The former companion now views you as an enemy. Therefore, don't expect them to consider your feelings or your petitions because you will be deeply disappointed, and your requests can trigger their hostility.

Handling your interactions in a business manner will give you more power. You will learn the art of staying calm and rational, know how to stick to the topic, and refuse to be sidetracked. Staying calm ensures that the narcissist is the one reacting emotionally and appears to be crazier than you are. The horrible and embarrassing behavior of the narcissist should not intimidate you because the truth about the behavior will present itself. You used to protect the narcissist by keeping such behaviors hidden, but it will not do you any good now. Their actions will greatly relieve your well-being and help quick recovery because the rest of the world will see the narcissist more authentically.

However, it would help if you did not make derogatory statements about the narcissist. Only speak of the facts without changing anything. Don't apologize to the narcissist; stop dismissing and explaining their rude and negative behavior. You should also not bad mouth the family and friends of the narcissist or your children. The best thing is to let people see how the narcissists acts when under stress for themselves.

10. Take the best possible care of yourself.

Focus on the best self-care by including exercise and healthy food in your daily schedule because they will make you feel more powerful, stop worrying and stand strong to your needs. Good care of your body helps improve your self-esteem and prepares you to handle other challenges. When you move your body during exercise, it will help you to balance breathing by bringing oxygen into your brain and getting your heart pumping. Such actions will ensure that you are not emotionally shutting down and don't enter depression. Go for a massage and jump into a hot tub or whatever makes you feel relaxed. Keeping a journal of your mind and feelings can also help recovery. When you put insights and experiences on a paper, it is surprisingly validating and calming.

Keeping a journal will help you discover what is confusing your life and realize what you can do about this huge post-divorce change. Additionally, keeping a journal helps trigger your memory because you will not easily forget and diminish the negative interactions with the narcissist.

At this stage, you should not be stingy with yourself; the best move is to invest in your health and healing. You should channel your money and time to services that give you good emotional care. There is no selfishness in taking care of yourself because it will someday pay off for your children, your friends and your loved ones who constantly worry about you.

11. Remember why the relationship needed to end and set clear boundaries.

When you get a narcissist, many problems come along, including superiority, entitlement, false image projection, inability to take responsibility, intense need for control etc. It is not your duty to comanage those issues. Your best behavior in love will not fix their behavior because they must notice the problem and work on changing it. When your partner is not interested in fulfilling your expectations and needs, the best recourse is ending the relationship. You can even go further by blocking the narcissist on all your social media platforms and ceasing communication.

They will not appreciate or accept your perception of the relationship because they will always defend their actions but remember they're no longer in a position to validate. Your truth is good enough. Your narcissist partner has the skills to generate self-doubt in you to shift blame, and therefore don't allow their manipulation to make you second guess your choice. Therefore, it is important to have automated tactics to soothe yourself and initiate self-care. It is difficult to stay in a relationship where you walk on eggshells to avoid potential anger or disapproval.

12. Understand why you found them attractive in the first place.

The beginning of a relationship with the narcissist will portray them as affectionate, captivating and attentive. Their charming nature can be very disorienting when you end things with them by realizing they're not who you thought they were when the undesirable narcissistic traits such as manipulation, entitlement and controlling behavior, lack of empathy and arrogance start to show up in their attractive traits I've already taken over you. Therefore, when you divorce the narcissist, you need to stay grounded in yourself and your new self-awareness.

An effective way to break this cycle is by looking at where it started. Check out yourself and identify the unconscious motives that influenced your partner selection. When you do such a reflection, you will find out about your sense of worth by selecting someone with a commanding presence.

Finally, from this reflection, you will know how to love yourself and honor your boundaries. You will realize how you don't want to be treated.

13. Avoid trying to rationalize.

Sometimes you start missing the narcissist and making excuses for their behavior by reinterpreting their lies, by tiptoeing around the self-delusion to maintain peace and justify staying with them. That's when you rationalize and say, "Oh, they're not so bad." Please do not fall for it. Remember why you left that marriage, and don't be manipulated into considering dating them again. Do not even try reaching them again.

14. Stop Updating yourself on their lives

If you are recovering from an abusive relationship with a narcissist, it is important to avoid keeping up with their lives. Trying to stay informed about what your ex is doing now and who they might be seeing or dating will only cause additional trauma, delaying your healing process. Not only is keeping tabs on your abuser's life going to keep you stuck in the past, but it can also trigger feelings of jealousy or sadness when you see that they seem to be living happily without you. After all, narcissists are very good at manipulating others, and they will likely post photos of new romantic partners just to try and make you feel bad.

Rather than getting stuck in a spiral of negative emotions by stalking your ex online or checking up on them in real life, it is better to focus on building a fulfilling life for yourself. This may involve reconnecting with old friends, trying new hobbies or activities, or establishing healthy boundaries with any toxic family members still in your life. By focusing on positive things and taking care of yourself first and foremost, you can begin to heal from the hurtful ways that a narcissistic abuser manipulated and controlled you in the past. And as time goes on, those wounds will slowly heal away until all that's left is happiness and joy.

15. Discover new ways to cope with anxiety

Since you have been with a narcissist, they probably have kept you on edge for years, and your nervous system could be firing along the lines. You will likely experience new stresses and fear when you leave, worsening your anxiety.

Additionally, you no longer have sex and therefore don't have the oxytocin and dopamine which were helping you to keep your head above water. Therefore exercises like dancing, breathing, yoga and swimming play a vital role in helping you cope with anxiety. Do exercise every day and every time you need it.

16. Be Mindful of the Relationships Effects on Your thinking

When you have experienced the pain of narcissistic abuse, it can be difficult to break free from the deep-rooted effects that linger within your psyche. However, with time and dedication, it is possible to overcome the negative behavior patterns that may have been engrained in you by your abuser.

To begin this process, it is important to be mindful of your actions and the way that you speak. By being careful and thinking critically before you act or speak, you can avoid falling back into old habits that might remind you of your abuser. With practice, over time you will be able to fully release yourself from the toxic grip of their influence and reclaim your own innate sense of self which is joy and pure love.

17. Don't blame yourself.

Now that you have realized that your ex was a narcissist and you know how unhealthy the patterns you participated in made you feel, you may assume that you allowed all these things to happen for a long time without stopping the narcissist. You may start wondering how you could be stupid, naive or gullible. Consequently, you will feel ashamed, especially when interacting with family and friends who were turned in long before you. Take it easy on yourself because narcissists know how to go about seduction tricks, and you are only human. Maybe you will have self-esteem issues that you need to examine when you get better, but you must forgive yourself. Console yourself that you are innocent, which is a good thing. You are someone with good intentions, trust and an open heart – something that narcissist can't match and will always struggling to have.

18. Focus on growing your self-love

The strategy of almost all narcissists is to downgrade you and upgrade themselves. Therefore, it is unlikely that you had any compliments, support or appreciation. Additionally, you may have been verbally and physically abused, and the narcissist aims to make your stay insecure in a foreign territory. Maybe you lost trust in your judgment after being gaslighted for a long. The best place to begin your healing process is

subscribing to self-help programs and groups to help you focus on self-love, which is important in restoring self-esteem post-divorce. Go for regular meetups with groups that work on the same type of personal growth you are interested in.

19. Prioritize your pleasure

Most dysfunctional relationships depend on sex because emotional fulfillment and intimacy are not always available. Narcissist well explores this tactic because they use sex as a powerful tool to feel needed. They always have a power-driven agenda behind maintaining your desire for sexual affection. Therefore, you may still want them sexually, even post-divorce. But how do you cope with this? Pick up a sex toy because that toy is devoid of human empathy, love, or even compassion, and it will help in healing your sexual self until you are ready for the next relationship.

20. Acknowledge your jealousy.

Many narcissists will replace you within days or weeks after breaking up. The people they move on with are those they have been keeping full-time when you two were in a relationship. The narcissist aims to ensure they have secured their supply and must have some energy source to feed on. By now, you know that the narcissist struggles to maintain healthy attachments and doesn't have authentic feelings of connection, and you might have been part of the arrangement that ceased to be convenient when you walked out of the abuse. Whoever falls into the trap next will be like a better business deal. When you start feeling jealous, you will keep in mind that whoever you are dating next is just someone who has no idea of the narcissist and has been set up the way you were set up, and the results will be the same in the long run. Therefore, it will be helpful to convert their jealousy into compassion for them.

21. Stop looking back.

By staying with a narcissist for a long time, you may look back and wonder why you wasted a lot of time with them. Additionally, if you did investments together or accumulated some debts and had kids with them, there is much more on your plate than wasted time.

The best action to take if you are in a toxic relationship is to get out of that toxic relationship. Try not to look back and focus on what is coming in the brighter future as much as possible. As the wise say, *it is not possible getting through a human life without regrets*.

22. Avoid Retaliation

Even when the narcissist makes great efforts to hurt you post-divorce, resist the urge to fight back. They are looking to hurt you so that you can respond and know they still have control over you. Continuing to engage only fuels more drama. Instead, if it looks impossible to avoid their tactics, focus on remaining as neutral as possible. If you need to vent, share your concerns with someone without any ties with the narcissist. The person cannot be a mutual friend because they may tell the narcissist what you say, or the narcissist may start triangulation tactics through the mutual friend.

23. Seek to Forgive Yourself

Anyone that falls into the trap of a narcissist can experience narcissistic abuse. It wasn't your fault that you were a victim of the abuse. Blaming yourself drags you back from moving on. Instead, start being compassionate and kind to yourself daily. Practicing self-forgiveness reinforces your emotional well-being and gives you healthier relationships and a more positive attitude.

24. **Take your time to heal before dating again.**

Your abuser may have been a romantic partner, but avoiding the temptation of distracting yourself with a new relationship is crucial. Take enough time to process what happened and realize how to be independent. You may be fragile right now, which increases your risk of attracting another narcissistic person. Therefore, focus on building a relationship with yourself and stop being a people pleaser. Allow yourself to grieve, grow stronger in self-love and reconnect with others who can support and love you.

These are the top 24 tips for toxic relationships recovery that your recovery process must focus on to see you start feeling happier.

Final Takeaway

Ending a relationship with a narcissist can be difficult, but it's not impossible because it's not easy to get over a narcissist. You will need to focus on yourself and your healing in order to move on. This means cutting off all communication with the narcissist, getting support from loved ones, and seeking therapy. Be mindful of your thoughts and how you talk to yourself and more.

Overcoming narcissistic abuse also requires that you stop blaming yourself, stop being worried over and over your failed relationship, learn how to be independent, and accept you can't do anything to change the narcissist's tactics. The tips discussed above will help you in healing your life, healing your body, healing your heart and generally help you in toxic relationship recovery. The abuse is not your fault; you can only stop it by leaving the relationship. Apply these tips to start total toxic relationships recovery process.

Narcissism abuse is more prevalent than we know. What if your friend is in this toxic relationship? Our next chapter will discuss what to do.

Chapter 9: What To Do If You Think Your Friend Might Be In A Toxic Relationship

We all have those friends we worry about. You know, the ones who always seem to be in bad relationships? The ones who never seem to be happy, no matter what they do or how hard they try? If you have a friend in a toxic relationship and believe that this relationship is not working well for them, it may not be easy to know what to do. However, if you are looking for a way to help a friend in an unhealthy relationship, there are different steps you can take to help them out. Keep reading for tips on how to support your friend and get them out of a bad situation.

1. Bring up the subject in a gentle way.

If you want to talk to your friend about their toxic relationship, don't go straight to calling them and asking about their relationship status or questioning them about their toxic partner. Try bringing it up gently. Begin by discussing general stuff they relate to, like movies, books, or songs about self-worth. You can then begin asking them about the topic in a manner that your friend might also relate to.

This approach will allow your friend to open up (at the correct time they are willing to) and you may be able to find out more about her/his relationship.

2. Give them a hug

Sometimes, your friend's only need is a tight hug when they start opening up to you. As much as it sounds very basic, it works. Before advising your friend in a toxic relationship, a hug will tell them that you are there for them.

According to science, a simple hug can help them mentally.

3. Listen to your friend with empathy.

A friend who confides in you about their toxic relationship needs an ear and a shoulder to cry on. It is, therefore, important to listen attentively without judging them. Give them time to express themselves freely, and don't interrupt. Additionally, don't make assumptions about the situation.

As you listen, it is important not to give unsolicited advice because it may make them think you're not taking them seriously. All you have to do is provide support and assurance that you're there for them.

The most important aspect is empathizing with them because it will help you connect with them deeper. It will also show your friend that you care about them and are ready to understand them. It also helps us to build trust and strengthen your relationships. It is also important to know that arguing is not listening because you can get pulled into the argument or try defending your friend. This should not happen; instead, let them take the lead in the conversation and listen without taking sides. If you try defending or rationalizing your partner's behavior, it will make them feel even worse.

4. Focus on the unhealthy behaviors

When you hold the conversation, focus on the unhealthy behaviors in your friend's relationship and aim at providing your friend with a safe space to talk about these behaviors. Sometimes, you may use your instinct to immediately brand the relationship as "abusive" so that your friend sees how severe the situation is. However, doing this will cause your friend to retreat and shut down.

Therefore, focus on the specific behaviors you have seen and find out how that behavior makes your friend feel. For example, you can say, "It looks like your partner is all over your back, always wanting to know where you are and always texting and calling – how does such a behavior make you feel?"

Additionally, you may gently point out that specific behaviors look unhealthy and give your honest opinion about how you would feel if someone did it to you. With these tactics, you will get your friend to understand that certain behaviors are appropriate and other behaviors are inappropriate in a relationship. Help them realize by themselves that something is wrong with their relationship and acknowledge that their feelings are legitimate.

5. **Offer support and understanding to your friend.**

Knowing how to help your friend in a toxic relationship might be difficult. You may feel like your comments on the situation might cause a fight but you want to support without making things worse. Offer support by assuring your friend that you're there for them and that you care about them.

If your friend is not able to speak to you, the best thing is to encourage them to seek professional help. However, remember they decide whether or not they want to leave the relationship. If they want the help of a professional, you can offer them a reference. There may also be an option where you may feel like you can provide practical help, like suggesting ways to step out of the relationship.

However much you feel they should leave the relationship, please don't force your opinion on them. You should also not give them advice unless they ask for it because it might make them feel more guilty.

6. Keep the conversation friendly, not a lecture

Only a few people in abusive relationships know that they are victims in the relationship, and it is more likely that they are unwilling to be viewed as victims. You can only be helpful by making yourself emotionally accessible to your friend. The best way to assure your friend that you are not judgmental of them is to normalize the conversation. You can talk openly about your own experiences with relationship troubles. This strategy will help your friend feel as though they are not alone. However, it would help if you did not derail the conversation, so keep focusing on your friend's situation. Try making it feel like an even exchange between two friends, not like a teacher -student or therapist and patient conversation.

7. Respect their boundaries

Your friend may want to talk about the relationship situation. When that happens, allow them and listen without judging. However, you may have seen that they are in a toxic relationship, but if they don't want to talk about it, respect their wishes. Don't try talking them out of their relationship or telling them what they should do because this can make things worse. Tell them how you feel about their situation but make it clear that your feelings are your own and you are just expressing them as opinions and not giving orders.

8. Expect more future conversations.

When you first have a conversation with your friend, they will admit a few things that happened, and they may suddenly pull away or take it back. Do not be very determined to get your friend to change their mind about their partner completely, and you don't need to press them hard so that they can "admit" that they are being abused. The conversation aims to show them that you care and they can talk to you any time. It is not guaranteed that the situation will be resolved perfectly after a single conversation, so expect to have more talks like this. Exercise patience throughout the process, and be satisfied that you are doing the right thing by having this conversation on this difficult topic.

9. Assure them of confidentiality.

Don't break their trust when your friend opens up with such information. They are entrusting you with this sensitive information, and the least you should do is keep the information private.

Don't go gossiping about it. Assure your friend that you will maintain their secret. Additionally, never mention their situation as a story with anonymous characters: for example, *"there is this person I know who went through this, but I can't name them. So, this is what happened to them...."* It would be best if you avoided these discussions because the ones you tell can track down those links and identify that friend. The promise that you will not disclose what they are going through gives them peace of mind.

10. Don't distance yourself.

Distancing yourself can be subtle at first and a natural reaction that you may take, but avoid changing the nature of your relationship because you dislike your friend's partner. You may not like the partner, but you must accept and tolerate that person.

If you care about your friend, you should prioritize your relationship with them above disliking their partner or relationship. After all, they may end their relationship tomorrow. You have been there for your friend and will be there long after. You may be the lifeline they need to regain their sanity, so don't cut the rope.

Final Takeaway

When you realize that your friend is caught in a toxic relationship, please resist the urge to judge before listening to them. When you talk to them, be available, and offer emotional support without forcing them with your decision. They are opening up because they only want your patient ear, not your decision on the matter. You can only encourage them to seek professional help, but if your friend is not willing to get professional help, be kind and loving to them until they are ready. With time, they will get the courage to do what they need to do and will need your support even more.

Chapter 10: Resources for People Who Need Help Dealing with a Narcissist and FAQ

In the United States, 15% of the population is likely to have NPD. Narcissistic personality disorder (NPD) makes people lack empathy, and such people display a high sense of superiority. The condition is more common in males than females but affects all genders. A person with such traits is a narcissist. Dealing with a narcissist requires setting boundaries, seeking education about narcissistic behaviors, and finding support groups and networks. This article will discuss some resources that will help you deal with a narcissist and some frequently asked questions.

Resources For People Who Need to Deal with A Narcissist

Many resources are available to help you deal with a narcissist. These resources include support groups, coaches, and helplines, among other resources, as shown below
.

1. The Narcissist Support Groups

A support group is a platform where survivors of narcissistic abuse come together to learn, share and heal. In this group, narcissistic abuse survivors are willing to help others find healing. When you join this group, you have a good chance of recovering from your experience with a narcissist and an opportunity to learn how to leave and live away from a narcissistic relationship. The support groups are safe spaces where you will meet people with similar experiences. The members will listen without judging you since they know that dealing with a narcissist can hurt someone. Here are some support groups:

- Survivors of Narcissistic Abuse & Codependency Support Group

This group is private, with 2,570 members, and they help people who have suffered from narcissistic abuse in both love and personal relationship. The group discusses and encourages through sharing of experiences as it also holds talks about bonding and trauma and provides support on how to break the cycle. Before signing up for any meeting, you MUST attend a First Timers Meeting event to ensure community safety, and there are NO exceptions to this rule. On their website, go to the "Events" section and sign up for a First Timers Group to attend the meeting before signing up for an Established Member meeting.

- Mensgroup.com

If you are a man who is a recovering victim of narcissistic behavior, it can be tough finding someone to talk to about your emotions, feelings, and trauma. Many people don't believe that men, too, can be victims of narcissistic relationships. Whether you have narcissistic parents, a narcissistic spouse or children with narcissism, this group is an all-man online platform where you can get the support you. The group believes anyone can heal, grow, and change with the right support. Access to this group will cost you $1 per day, and you can leave the group when you want. Getting a support system from fellow men can help you overcome your trauma and lead a healthy, successful, and happy life.

2. Associations To Help Deal with A Narcissist

1) National Domestic Violence Hotline:

This hotline organization offers hotline texting and online chat for people in narcissistic relationships who need support getting out of these unsafe relationships and for people looking for help to recover from narcissistic relationships. They have tools on their website to help you get resources, such as support groups, in your locality.

2) I Believe Your Abuse:

This online guide offers narcissistic survivors a chance to recover from narcissistic abuse. The group offers a list of therapy and support group resources organized by state. I Believe Your Abuse offers email/text/Skype sessions from professionals specializing in narcissistic abuse recovery. Complete the contact form on this site to get started, or contact ibelieveyourabuse@gmail.com to access the support groups.

3. Find Help from Coaching.

There are groups like QueenBeeing.com for both men and women recovering from narcissistic abuse. This group has certified life coaches and a survivor of narcissistic abuse. Their team of certified life coaches is ready to help you during and after your narcissistic abuse recovery. The coaches and counselors of this group are trauma-informed and trauma-sensitive. You can choose how personal you want – from telephone, text or messenger coaching to email coaching – and they also offer lower-cost group coaching and many free options for peer group support. Additionally, they have a legal expert on their team who can offer you legal help and advice with divorce and other legal issues faced by narcissistic abuse survivors. You can contact them through their official email QueenBeeingTeam@gmail.com.

Frequently Asked Questions About Narcissism

1. Is There Healthy Narcissism?

Healthy narcissism is a form of narcissism that does not hurt someone- which is perceived as an outstanding trait. For example, the need to prove to others that your skills, your personality, and your abilities are worthy of their attention or the enjoyment of getting others to want to see you or getting others to notice you are considered healthy narcissism. Healthy narcissism is just a healthy motivation to show off and to have people meet your needs to take care of some psychological function. There is nothing wrong with it. Some of us should do it more often. So, healthy narcissism is simply paying attention to your own needs without focusing on others, feeling good about it, and no one's getting hurt.

2. What Kind of Partner Does A Narcissist Target?

Nearly all nnarcissists like finding partners willing to sacrifice their happiness for the narcissist's happiness. The nnarcissist has no desire to focus on the victim's needs. They like a partner who is not very demanding, a people pleaser, loyal and persevering of their abuse, and someone who is not very confident in themselves they can easily manipulate. This partner will easily provide the supply of demands and needs they have without too many problems.

3. What Is A Narcissistic Apology?

A narcissistic apology is a form of apology characterized by insincerity to make the recipient feel guilty for the original inflictions done to them. Any apology that leaves the victim feeling guilty is not genuine. An example of such an apology is: *"I am sorry I was only joking," "I'm sorry if you got that turned out as offensive,"* or *"you are acting too sensitive."* Such an apology may be a form of gaslighting.

4. What Are the Types Of Narcissism?

There are two different types of narcissism which include <u>overt and covert</u> narcissism. Individuals with overt NPD express a more outgoing, charming, and self-confident personality. In addition, they may seek outward forms of success and approval. On the other hand, people with <u>covert NPD</u> are more insecure, anxious, and sensitive. They habitually exaggerate their abilities and seek social validation, but their narcissistic traits may be less noticeable.

5. Do Narcissists Know They Are Gaslighting?

Some people diagnosed with NPD <u>may engage in</u> manipulative behaviors, such as gaslighting, when someone makes another person question their reality or sanity. If a person knows that they have NPD, they may well understand their behavior during therapy. If they are unaware of the NPD condition, they may not know they are being manipulative or gaslighting.

Final Takeaway

The fact remains that you are not to blame for the narcissistic abuse that you went through. The toxicity of narcissistic abuse can scramble your sense of reality. Finding support from your community, groups, peers, coaches, and mental health professionals like therapists can greatly support your recovery journey from abuse and knowing how to deal with a narcissist. We have covered some top resources like narcissist support groups, associations that help deal with narcissists and frequently asked questions. Consider finding help from the support resources in this chapter. You must realize that you are not alone and that it is possible to find your self-worth once again! You got this!

Conclusion

Dealing with a narcissistic relationship can be a challenging and emotionally draining experience. In order to identify and cope with a narcissist at work, at home, and in our social lives, it is important to be aware of the key signs commonly exhibited by these individuals. For example, narcissists are often overly-competitive and focused on achieving their own goals without regard for others; they may also exhibit grandiose attitudes, such as an inflated sense of self-worth or importance or an unrealistic belief that they are always right.

Other than being able to recognize the signs of a narcissistic relationship, it is also important to understand the negative effects that can arise from this type of toxic connection. These relationships may cause feelings of depression or anxiety as well as feelings of resentment or confusion. Furthermore, children raised in a narcissistic family environment may struggle with issues related to trust and self-esteem as they grow up.

While there may be no easy solutions when dealing with a narcissistic relationship on any level - professional, personal, or social, it is important to build up your own resilience and self-confidence so that you can maintain positive relationships with others, even during difficult times. You can also seek support from friends and family members who will provide you with the emotional strength and guidance you need to leave the relationship.

And if you find yourself struggling with depression or anxiety due to your narcissistic relationship, seeking professional help from a therapist or counselor can be an incredibly effective way to recover from these negative effects.

By following the strategies given to leave and thrive after a relationship, with time and effort, you can overcome challenges posed by a narcissist and move forward in your life stronger than ever before!

Thank You for Reading!

For more books, please follow me here

(social media handles)

References

Chua, R. M. (1970, January 1). Come down the tree of narcissism; go up the tree of salvation. Come down the Tree of Narcissism; Go up the Tree of Salvation. Retrieved October 30, 2022, from http://michaelckw.blogspot.com/2013/11/come-down-tree-of-narcissism-go-up-tree.html

Lowery, T. (2018, March 9). Narcissists on social media - how to spot and avoid them. LinkedIn. Retrieved October 30, 2022, from https://www.linkedin.com/pulse/narcissists-social-media-how-spot-avoid-them-tom-lowery

Hmaker, S. (2015, March 11). 7 ways to nip narcissism in the bud [Review of 7 ways to nip narcissism in the bud]. Https://Www.washingtonpost.com/; The Washington Post. https://www.washingtonpost.com/news/parenting/wp/2015/03/11/7-ways-to-nip-narcissism-in-the-bud/

Hallman, L. (2022, March 3). 15 Signs of a Narcissistic Boss & 10 Ways to Deal With Them (N. Saleh, Ed.) [Review of 15 Signs of a Narcissistic Boss & 10 Ways to Deal With Them]. Https://Www.choosingtherapy.com/; Choosing Therapy. https://www.choosingtherapy.com/narcissistic-boss/

ChoosingTherapy.com. (2022, October 11). Signs of a Narcissist Coworker & How to Deal With Them. Choosing Therapy. https://www.choosingtherapy.com/narcissist-coworker/

Kassel, G. (2022, May 1). 9 Signs You're Dating a Narcissist — and How to Get Out. Healthline. https://www.healthline.com/health/mental-health/am-i-dating-a-narcissist

Arzt, N. (2021, December 15). *12 Tips for Living With a Narcissist*. Retrieved from Choosing Therapy: https://www.choosingtherapy.com/living-with-a-narcissist/

Robinson, K. M. (n.d.). *How to Handle a Narcissist*. Retrieved from WebMD: https://www.webmd.com/mental-health/features/handle-narcissist

Scala, V. (2021, December 8). *8 TIPS FOR DEALING WITH A NARCISSIST*. Retrieved from Anchor
Therapy LLC:
https://www.anchortherapy.org/blog/8-tips-for-dealing-with-a-narcissist-nj-nyc

Shull, M. (n.d.). *How to Cope When You Love a Narcissist*. Retrieved from Mary Shull:
https://www.maryshull.com/blog/how-to-cope-when-you-love-a-narcissist/

Thomas, N. (2021, September 24). *13 Tips for How to Deal With a Narcissist*. Retrieved from
Choosing Therapy: https://www.choosingtherapy.com/deal-with-narcissist/

Dawson, K. (n.d.). *How to Leave a Toxic Relationship, According to a Psychologist*. Retrieved
from BRIDES: https://www.brides.com/how-to-leave-a-toxic-relationship-5105346

Feuerman, M. (2022, October 12). *6 Steps to Leave a Toxic Relationship*. Retrieved from
verywellmind: https://www.verywellmind.com/how-to-leave-a-toxic-marriage-4091900

Laderer, A. (2022, July 8). *8 steps to safely and conclusively end a toxic relationship, according to
couples therapists*. Retrieved from Insider:
https://www.insider.com/guides/health/sex-relationships/how-to-leave-a-toxic-relations
hip

Lamoreux, K. (2021, July 21). *10 Pointers for Ending Toxic Relationships*. Retrieved from
PsychCentral: https://psychcentral.com/blog/steps-to-end-a-toxic-relationship

Rahman, I. (2022, August 29). *How to Leave a Toxic Relationship*. Retrieved from Choosing
therapy: https://www.choosingtherapy.com/how-to-leave-a-toxic-relationship/

Atkinson, A. (n.d.). *Narcissistic Abuse in a Toxic Relationship: This is What Happens to You*.
Retrieved from The QueenBeeing:
https://queenbeeing.com/narcissistic-abuse-in-a-toxic-relationship-this-is-what-happens
-to-you/

Brothwell, J. (2021, June 4). *9 Signs Of Narcissistic Abuse, Explained By A Therapist*. Retrieved from Your tango:
https://www.yourtango.com/experts/joanne-brothwell/9-signs-toxic-relationship-suffering-narcissistic-abuse

Dodgson, L. (2018, December 17). *8 things that can keep you trapped in a relationship with a narcissist*. Retrieved from Insider:
https://www.insider.com/things-that-trap-you-in-relationship-with-narcissist-2018-12

Gaba, S. (2021, June 21). *The Effects of Narcissistic Supply in a Toxic Relationship*. Retrieved from Psychology Today:
https://www.psychologytoday.com/us/blog/addiction-and-recovery/202106/the-effects-narcissistic-supply-in-toxic-relationship

Reid, A. J. (2021, December 9). *Power of You: How to Identify and Leave a Toxic, Narcissistic Relationship*. Retrieved from THE LUMINARIES MAGAZINE:
https://www.theluminariesmagazine.com/domestic-violence-lockdown-and-how-to-leave-a-toxic-narcissistic-relationship/

Jacquelyn Johnson, P. (2022, July 28). *All about narcissistic personality disorder*. Retrieved from MedicalNewsToday: https://www.medicalnewstoday.com/articles/9741

Kubala, K. (2022, August 18). *9 Tips for Dealing with Someone's Narcissistic Personality Traits*. Retrieved from healthline:
https://www.healthline.com/health/how-to-deal-with-a-narcissist

Schwartz, B. (2022, July 7). *Narcissistic Depression: Signs, Risk Factors & Treatment*. Retrieved from Choosing Therapy: https://www.choosingtherapy.com/narcissistic-depression/

Wade, D. (2022, January 19). *12 Signs You've Experienced Narcissistic Abuse (Plus How to Get Help)*. Retrieved from healthline:
https://www.healthline.com/health/narcissistic-victim-syndrome#false-perfection

Windermere, A. (n.d.). *Narcissistic Personality Disorder: How to Recognize Narcissism and Protect Your Mental Health*. Retrieved from HealthCentral: https://www.healthcentral.com/article/narcissistic-personality-disorder-how-to-recognize-narcissism-and-protect-your-mental-health

www.ingramcontent.com/pod-product-compliance
Lightning Source LLC
Chambersburg PA
CBHW070635030426
42337CB00020B/4029